NATIONAL
GEOGRAPHIC
KiDS

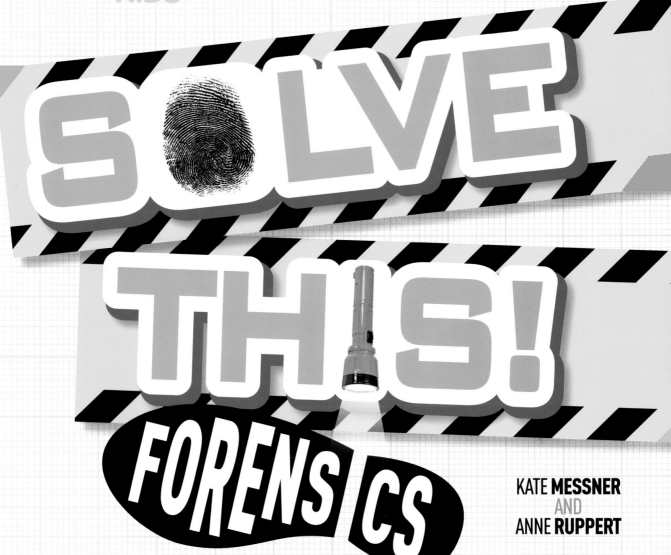

SOLVE THIS!

FORENSICS

KATE **MESSNER**
AND
ANNE **RUPPERT**

SUPER SCIENCE AND CURIOUS CAPERS FOR THE DARING DETECTIVE IN YOU

NATIONAL GEOGRAPHIC
WASHINGTON, D.C.

>> CONTENTS

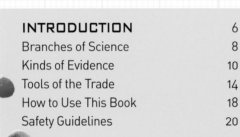

Mystery #1

Mystery #2

A DARK, RAINY NIGHT.
A BROKEN WINDOW.
STOLEN JEWELS.
NOT A SINGLE WITNESS.

BUT THE STORY OF THE HEIST IS WRITTEN ALL OVER THIS CRIME SCENE—IF YOU KNOW HOW TO READ IT.

It's a story written in mud and maggots, bite marks and blood, shoeprints, fingerprints, and everything in between. People who are specially trained to read and study the stories left behind at crime scenes are called forensic scientists. They collect, preserve, analyze, and interpret scientific evidence connected to a crime. Looked at all together, that evidence helps tell the story of what happened—and makes it more likely that the story will end with a suspect's arrest.

You've likely read a book or watched a television show or movie in which police investigators talk about collecting evidence. The most commonly talked about clues are probably fingerprints, left behind when the unique pattern of ridges on a person's fingertip is transferred to a surface, thanks to the sweat and oils that our bodies produce. Those impressions can be checked against databases of people who have been fingerprinted in their lifetimes to try and find a match. You probably know that blood, saliva, or hair left behind at a crime scene can also be matched to suspects sometimes, based on DNA—the genetic code we all carry that's even more unique to us than a fingerprint.

But did you know that tools, clothing, and batches of paint all have fingerprints of their own? That computers can be searched for hidden files even after a suspect deletes the evidence? Or that creepy-crawly insects can help detectives pinpoint when a crime probably took place?

That's why forensic experts need to be students of virtually every branch of science—human biology, zoology, chemistry, physics, entomology, botany, and computer science, too.

BRANCHES OF SCIENCE

Scientists are often SPECIALISTS, focusing on one of the following AREAS OF STUDY:

BOTANY,
the study of plants

BIOLOGY,
the study of living things
and how they interact

CHEMISTRY,
the study of
matter and
how chemical
reactions occur

GEOLOGY,
the study of Earth, what it is made of, and how it changes over time

ECOLOGY,
the study of where organisms live, how many there are, and how they are affected by their environment

METEOROLOGY,
the study of the atmosphere and weather

ZOOLOGY,
a branch of biology that specializes in the animal kingdom

OCEANOGRAPHY,
the study of Earth's oceans and seas

Some sciences are specific to FORENSIC SCIENCE:

FORENSIC ANTHROPOLOGY: the study of skeletal remains to help solve a crime

FORENSIC CHEMISTRY: chemical analysis of substances, including drugs

FORENSIC ENTOMOLOGY: the study of insects as they relate to solving a crime

FORENSIC ODONTOLOGY: the practice of matching dental details to individuals or their remains

FORENSIC PSYCHIATRY/ PROFILING: the study of the psychology of criminal behavior

KINDS OF EVIDENCE

Blood evidence

BLOOD CAN BE ANALYZED MANY DIFFERENT WAYS: for DNA, blood type, and as part of a blood spatter analysis (when an investigator studies patterns of blood on a surface to determine exactly where the victim and suspect were during the crime). A DNA test would make this type of evidence unique to one individual, but blood type and blood spatter analysis would need other supporting evidence to identify a suspect.

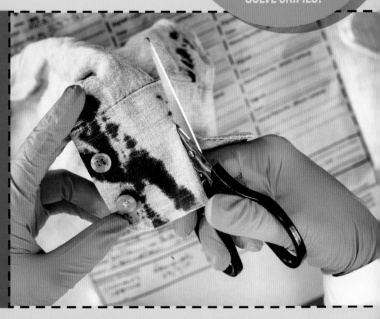

DNA

WHEN IT COMES TO A CRIME SCENE, YOU PROBABLY ASSOCIATE DNA WITH BLOOD. But our genetic code can be found in more than just blood! Any undamaged cell would still hold its DNA, so forensic scientists also look at cells present in saliva and hair found at crime scenes.

Insect evidence

INSECTS AREN'T USUALLY ACCUSED OF COMMITTING CRIMES, BUT THEY CAN HELP YOU ESTABLISH A TIMELINE FOR ONE. When scientists discover decaying matter that's related to a crime, they look for insects on it. By examining the insects, forensic scientists can often narrow down when the crime happened. That's because insects live a very predictable life cycle. Some insects, such as maggots, are born and grow on dead matter. If those insects are found on a dead person or animal related to a crime, scientists can look at how old the insects are to learn how long the person or animal has been dead (and therefore when the crime might have happened).

Fingerprints

You'd look for these after a break-in or burglary, often exposing them with dusting powders or chemicals. **EACH FINGER-PRINT IS UNIQUE TO ONE INDIVIDUAL!**

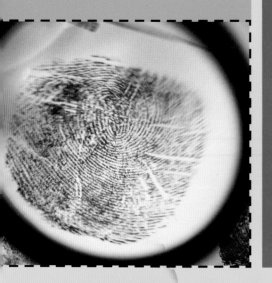

Handwriting

A note or other handwritten evidence at the scene of a crime can be used to rule out a suspect whose handwriting is totally different—or to point to one whose writing is a match. But be careful; it is possible for a suspect to change the way they write! **INVESTIGATORS HAVE TO BE SURE TO GET AN AUTHENTIC EXEMPLAR, OR HAND-WRITING SAMPLE, FOR THE COMPARISON.**

✿ Continued on the next page. ✿

Shoeprints or tire prints

These marks left behind by shoes or tires CAN BE USED TO PLACE A SUSPECT AT THE SCENE OF A CRIME! Prints left behind in dirt or mud can be preserved by making a cast of the impression.

Toxicology

THIS TYPE OF EVIDENCE HAS TO DO WITH THE CHEMICAL MAKEUP OF SUBSTANCES. A toxicology analysis can be used to determine if drugs or other chemicals are present in a sample. Chemical analysis can be used to investigate other materials, including paints and inks.

Skid marks

Scientists look at these when trying to figure out how an accident involving a car or bicycle might have occurred. These marks CAN HELP DETERMINE HOW FAST A VEHICLE MIGHT HAVE BEEN GOING, OR IN WHAT DIRECTION.

Skeletal remains

The bones of a skeleton might give some clues as to what the living person looked like. Layering clay onto the facial bones, for example, **GIVES HINTS AS TO WHAT A FACE MIGHT HAVE LOOKED LIKE.** You can even tell what the person's life might have been like by looking for clues in the bones that tell age, sex, and whether any of the bones were ever broken.

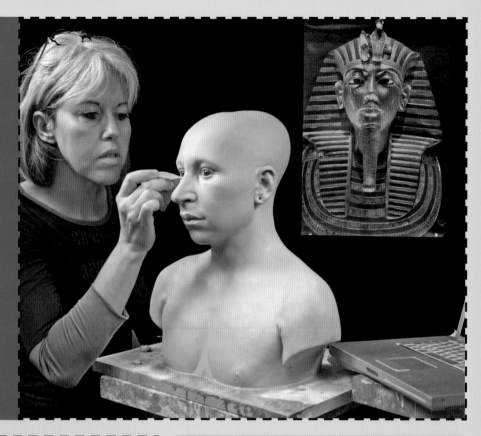

Toolmarks

THIS EVIDENCE APPEARS AS MARKS LEFT BY TOOLS THAT WERE USED IN A CRIME. You'd check for these after a break-in, perhaps matching marks left on wood, metal, or other material with the shape and pattern of a tool that may have been used to commit the crime. Marks can also be left on the tools themselves, so experts can match crime scene paint (from a door or maybe a window) to paint left on a crowbar, hammer, or screwdriver.

Trace evidence

THIS TYPE OF EVIDENCE IS SO TINY THAT IT'S CALLED A TRACE. It can include things such as hair, clothing fibers or threads, pollen, and even soil. While trace evidence is not usually unique to one individual (since it tends to have less detail than, say, fingerprints), it can be used to help place a suspect at the scene of a crime.

TOOLS OF THE TRADE

Advances in technology have been a great help to the field of forensic science. Here are some of the tools:

AFIS (Automated Fingerprint Identification System)

THIS COMPUTER DATABASE HOLDS FINGERPRINTS FROM EVERYONE IN THE UNITED STATES WHO HAS BEEN ARRESTED, AS WELL AS SOME INTERNATIONAL SUSPECTS, and millions of people who are fingerprinted for work or other reasons. The FBI has been updating AFIS for more than 60 years, and during that time, no two fingerprints have been found to be exactly the same. Only detectives, forensic scientists, and crime scene investigators have access to this database.

Crime scene investigation kit

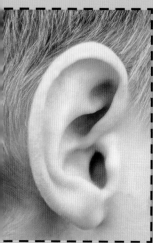

FearID ear print database

This collection of ear prints began with FearID, the Forensic Ear Identification research project, in Europe. **IT'S USED TO MATCH KNOWN EAR PRINTS FROM VOLUNTEERS AND CONVICTED CRIMINALS TO EAR PRINTS FOUND AT THE SCENE OF A CRIME.**

Protective gear

FORENSIC SCIENTISTS UNDERSTAND THE IMPORTANCE OF SAFETY PRACTICES. They wear gloves while collecting evidence. In the lab, they wear gloves and a lab coat, as well as safety goggles for any procedure that might result in fumes or splashes to the face.

✷ Continued on the next page. ✷

GC-MS (gas chromatograph-mass spectrometer)

THIS INSTRUMENT BREAKS DOWN A MYSTERY SUBSTANCE INTO ITS CHEMICAL PARTS. THEN IT COMPARES THE PARTS TO A LIBRARY OF KNOWN SUBSTANCES. That helps scientists find out what the mystery substance is. This process starts when the unknown substance is injected into the instrument. A "carrier gas" (usually helium) sweeps it into a long, coiled tube inside a warm oven, like wind blowing water in a puddle. In the oven, the sample continues to move along its journey and begins to separate into its components. As the mixture is separated, it arrives at a detector, where it's broken apart. Each compound breaks apart the same unique way every time. A graph is created to show the result of the chemical separation and fragmentation. Information from that graph can then be matched to a computerized library of known substances to identify the substance in question. This can be done with everything from paint samples and unknown powders to blood that might contain some kind of drug or poison.

FTIR
(Fourier transform infrared) spectrometer

THIS INSTRUMENT EXPOSES UNKNOWN SUBSTANCES TO INFRARED LIGHT, CREATES A GRAPH OF HOW THE SAMPLE INTERACTS WITH IT, and compares that graph to a library of known materials. This process, called infrared spectroscopy, can be used with liquids, powders, and solids.

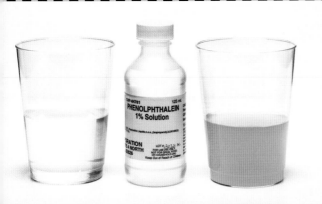

Phenolphthalein testing

THIS PROCESS IS USED TO CHECK A SAMPLE TO FIND OUT IF IT'S BLOOD. Phenolphthalein is an indicator, a substance that turns a specific color in the presence of a certain material. In this case, phenolphthalein turns hot pink when real blood is present. This blood-confirmation test is actually a two-step process that also requires hydrogen peroxide. (You might have heard of that because it's often used to sterilize wounds and keep them from getting infected.) In this situation, though, the hydrogen peroxide is used to create a chemical reaction. Red blood cells contain a substance called hemoglobin, which reacts with hydrogen peroxide when the two substances are put together to form a new substance. That new substance reacts with the phenolphthalein to create the hot pink color that lets you know that blood is present.

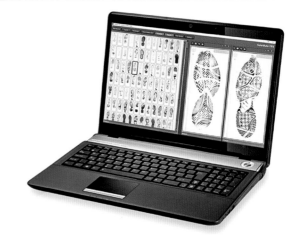

Shoeprint database

THIS FOOTWEAR DATABASE WAS DESIGNED TO COMPARE A CRIME SCENE SHOEPRINT TO KNOWN FOOTWEAR IMAGES to help determine the make and model of the shoe that left the print. Investigators enter the measurements of the print and an image, and the database comes back with information about the shoe.

HOW TO USE THIS BOOK

NOW THAT YOU KNOW THE BASICS OF FORENSIC SCIENCE AND CRIME SCENE INVESTIGATION, IT'S TIME TO PUT THAT KNOWLEDGE TO WORK SOLVING SOME MYSTERIES!

In the pages that follow, you'll find four crime scene scenarios, complete with suspects and evidence. For each imaginary crime, you'll find the following:

THE CRIME SCENE
Pay close attention to details when you study this. You never know where an important clue might turn up!

1

SITUATION NOTES
These notes explain what's happened, whether it's a break-in, kidnapping, or heist.

2

THE SCENARIO

SITUATION NOTES:

A rare plant from the Australian outback has been stolen from a university greenhouse, where it was being studied by botany professor Chet Redwood. Acacia ixiophylla, commonly known as the sticky wattle, is a shrub believed to have tumor-fighting properties. Redwood was hoping to study the plant's potential uses in fighting cancer.

UNIVERSITY GREENHOUSE

DO NOT CROSS

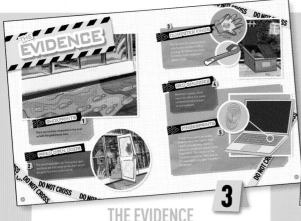

THE EVIDENCE

What's been collected from the crime scene?
This might be anything from fingerprints
to blood to tiny traces of soil or pollen.
But remember that not all evidence turns
out to be helpful. It takes more than one
clue to tie a suspect to the crime.

THE SUSPECTS

Who might have committed this crime?
Who had the opportunity and the motive?
Your suspect notes will include details about
each person's background and possible motives
as well as notes on where they were around
the time that the crime was committed.

INVESTIGATING THE EVIDENCE

A closer look at the evidence, how it's
processed, studied, and analyzed, and how
it might help to prove that a suspect
did—or didn't—commit the crime.

LET'S REVIEW

Check this quick overview of the suspects, motives,
and evidence. This is the last section you'll read
before you turn the page to learn the solution,
so take your time here. Review your notes
and decide who you think the real culprit is.
Then, turn the page to learn ...

THE SOLUTION

Discover who really
committed the crime
and how forensic science
helped to crack the case.

You might want to have a notebook or
piece of scrap paper handy so you can
jot down notes as you work your way
through each mystery. **DON'T READ
AHEAD! TRY TO SOLVE THE
MYSTERY YOURSELF BEFORE
YOU PEEK AT THE SOLUTION.**

TRY IT YOURSELF!

THE MOCK CRIMES AND FORENSIC INVESTIGATIONS IN THIS BOOK HAVE BEEN DESIGNED TO GET YOUR IMAGINATION INVOLVED IN FUN, CREATIVE, AND CHALLENGING WAYS.

The scientific tests and experiments described in the book are conducted by professional and highly trained forensic investigators. As some of the tests involve the use of blood samples, chemicals, and other materials that would require special handling, never attempt to conduct these experiments. Instead, we have included some experiments that you can do to explore your newly learned forensic investigation skills. These experiments are all labeled as "TRY THIS!"

TRY THIS!

DISCOVER HOW AN ACCELERATED MASS SPECTROMETER WORKS

An accelerated mass spectrometer is essential in the process of carbon dating because it separates carbon-14 and carbon-12 particles. That allows scientists to count them and determine the ratio between the two. Here's a fun experiment you can try at home to see how this machine works.

>> WHAT YOU'LL NEED

- a three-ring binder and two hardcover books with flat spines
- A hair dryer
- Books, rulers, or other materials to create a wall
- About 30 pennies (representing carbon-12)
- About 15 nickels (representing carbon-14)

ADULT SUPERVISION REQUIRED: Use of hot-air source

>> PROCEDURE

1. Place the binder on a hard, flat surface like a table or wooden floor to make a ramp. Be sure to set it up near an electrical outlet.

2. Place the two books on the ramp, spines facing each other, and spaced apart just enough to insert a coin to roll down the ramp.

3. Plug in your hair dryer and lay it on its side so that it's blowing across the path the coins will take after they roll down the ramp. It should be six to eight inches (15 to 20 cm) past the end of the ramp. The hair dryer will be blowing the coins off to the side after they leave the ramp.

4. Set up a little wall or blockade of some kind a few feet away to stop the coins after they've turned. A row of books or rulers will work fine for this.

5. Turn on the hair dryer and, one by one, roll your coins on their edge down the ramp. The force of the air coming from the hair dryer will cause the coins to turn.

6. When you're out of coins, check out the two piles. Did one kind of coin usually turn before the other? Which turned more quickly? What might account for this?

>> HOW IT WORKS

You'll find that the pennies, which are lighter than the nickels, turn sooner. The heavier nickels will take a little longer to turn, so this process separates the coins into piles based on their weight. The same thing happens in a mass spectrometer, which uses an electric field to accelerate the particles and a magnetic field to cause them to turn. In your simulation, the acceleration comes from the force of gravity as the coins roll down the ramp. Your hair dryer takes the place of the magnetic field, causing the coins to turn and separate by weight.

- About 30 pennies (representing cart
- About 15 nickels (representing carbc

SAFETY FIRST!

Some of the Try This activities in this book require the use of heat sources, sharp objects, or other procedures that require an adult's help. Look for these notes throughout, then go grab an adult to join the fun!

Please read and follow the below SAFETY GUIDELINES with an adult before you perform any of the experiments in this book. Make sure to follow these rules as you work through the experiments!

1. BE CAREFUL during the experiments, and use extra caution when working with flames, chemicals, sharp knives or scissors, or hot objects.

2. PREPARE YOURSELF to work in a safe manner (for example: wear safety goggles when working with chemicals or projectiles, chemical safety gloves when working with chemicals, heat–resistant mitts when working with hot objects, no loose clothes or loose hair when working with flames).

3. CREATE A SAFE WORK SPACE (for example: keep paper or other combustible items away when working with heat or flames, no food or beverages in your work area, choose an area with appropriate ventilation if you're using chemicals, and choose an area that younger children or a pet cannot unexpectedly enter).

4. HAVE SAFETY EQUIPMENT NEARBY (for example: have a fire extinguisher, baking soda, or other fire response tool nearby when working with flames; have a first aid kit nearby).

5. WASH AND DRY YOUR HANDS before and after each experiment.

6. FOLLOW the DIRECTIONS for each experiment and TAKE YOUR TIME.

7. READ and FOLLOW THE SAFETY TIPS in this book and the guidelines on all product labels, and use your own common sense and judgment.

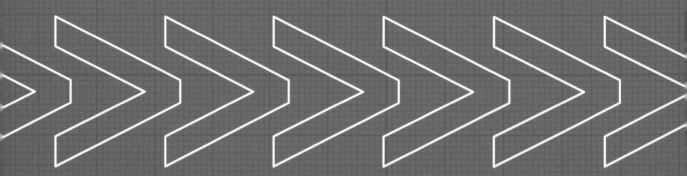

Mystery #1

STOLEN SPECIES

MISSING

THE SCENARIO

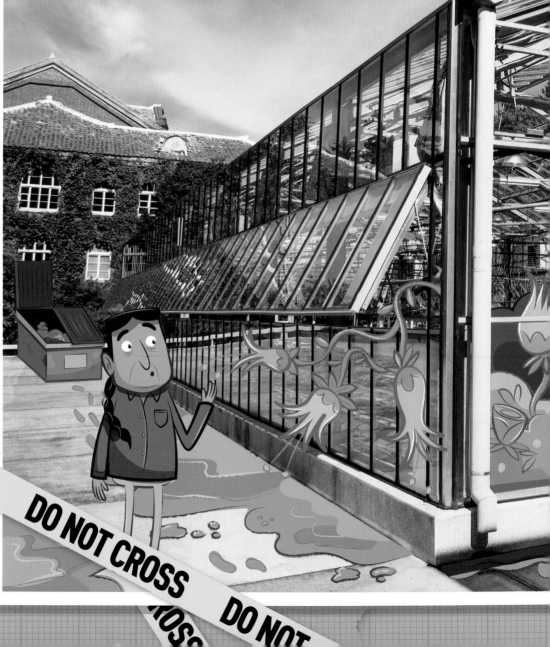

DO NOT CROSS DO NOT CROSS DO NOT CROSS DO NOT

SITUATION NOTES:

A rare plant from the Australian outback has been stolen from a university greenhouse, where it was being studied by botany professor Chet Redwood. *Acacia ixiophylla*, commonly known as the sticky wattle, is a shrub believed to have tumor-fighting properties. Redwood was hoping to study the plant's potential uses in fighting cancer.

THE EVIDENCE

SHOEPRINTS **1**

There are multiple shoeprints in the mud outside the greenhouse door.

PRIED OPEN DOOR

2 The greenhouse door has been pried open, and there are toolmarks on the door where the paint has been scratched off.

DO NOT CROSS DO NOT CROSS DO NOT CROSS DO NOT

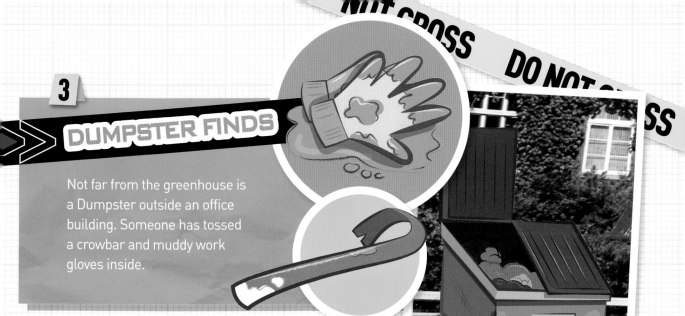

3 DUMPSTER FINDS

Not far from the greenhouse is a Dumpster outside an office building. Someone has tossed a crowbar and muddy work gloves inside.

RED SMUDGES 4

Redwood's laptop, which was in his office, has some unidentified red smudges on the keyboard.

FINGERPRINTS

5

Though there aren't any visible fingerprints on the laptop, if the culprit accessed data, there's a chance he or she left behind some fingerprints. The crowbar in the Dumpster is another likely source, if it was used to pry open the green-house door.

THE SUSPECTS

WHO WOULD WANT TO STEAL A PLANT? **DETECTIVES INTERVIEWED REDWOOD AND OTHERS AND CAME UP WITH A LIST OF POSSIBLE SUSPECTS:**

MOTIVE: *Money*

Longo tried to purchase the plant for her company's research project and was upset when the university was unwilling to part with it.

MAVIS LONGO,
a visiting pharmaceutical company researcher

DO NOT CROSS

FINN JAMISON,
a botany student minoring in
computer science

MOTIVE: Prestige

Jamison is an intern at the city's
botanical garden and may have
stolen the plant to pass off as his own
discovery and donate to the garden.

MOTIVE: Jealousy

Linnaeus is a rival of Redwood. He
was also in Australia searching for
new species at the time Redwood
found the sticky wattle.

SVEN LINNAEUS,
another university botany professor

DR. JARRETT WASHINGTON,
Redwood's supervisor

MOTIVE: Job security

There's been talk of replacing
Washington as botany department
chairperson, so claiming a research
breakthrough on such a rare plant
could help him stay in a leadership
role in the department.

DO NOT CROSS

BLOOD ANALYSIS

>>> **THE RED SMUDGES FOUND ON REDWOOD'S KEYBOARD ARE YOUR FIRST ORDER OF BUSINESS.** Since there's broken glass at the greenhouse crime scene, there's a possibility the person who broke in may have been injured. If those smudges on the keyboard are blood, you might have DNA evidence connecting the thief to the crime. Carefully, you place the laptop in an evidence bag and take it to the lab.

DNA AND CELLS

To understand DNA, you need to know a little about cells. All living things are made up of tiny, micro-scopic building blocks called cells. All cells have a nucleus, or control center, and inside that nucleus are chromosomes. Chromosomes are threadlike structures made of DNA (short for deoxyribonucleic acid), and they're responsible for passing down traits—things like eye color and hair color in humans—from one generation to the next.

Each individual living organism, whether it's a plant, animal, or single-celled life-form, has a unique code of DNA. That's why DNA can be so helpful in investigating crimes.

Illustration of a DNA strand

DNA FINGERPRINTING

No two people have exactly the same DNA in their cells, so it's possible to match DNA from a crime scene to a DNA sample taken from a suspect to find out if they match. We call this process DNA fingerprinting, because like fingerprints, DNA is unique to each person.

The forensic blood analysis lab is where scientists work on many different kinds of blood investigations. They analyze DNA and study blood spatter patterns to give detectives an idea of how a crime happened or in what direction a suspect may have fled. Scientists here also do testing to find out whether or not a stain is blood. That's where you'll need to start with the red smudges on the keyboard.

TESTING A SAMPLE

» You give the laptop to an analyst, who begins by moistening a cotton swab with sterile saline. That's a specially balanced salt-and-water solution used to lift blood samples from an object without destroying or damaging the blood cells, which might be needed later to test for DNA. Then she rolls the swab gently onto a red-stained area of the computer's space bar. You see that some of the red substance is now on the cotton.

» Next, she needs to find a vial of phenolphthalein, an indicator that turns hot pink when blood is present. She puts a few drops of phenolphthalein onto the red part of the swab.

» Carefully, she adds two drops of hydrogen peroxide to the swab ...

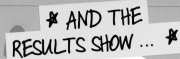

✻ AND THE RESULTS SHOW ... ✻

NOTHING HAPPENS. **THE SWAB LOOKS THE SAME. THERE'S NO HOT PINK COLOR, WHICH MEANS** THERE'S NO BLOOD. **THAT MEANS THERE CAN BE NO DNA ANALYSIS.**

But what could that red stuff be? Before you put the laptop back in its evidence bag, you lift it to your nose and take a sniff. It smells a whole lot like strawberry jam.

✻ Time to go back to the forensics drawing board and look at a different kind of evidence. ✻

FINGERPRINT ANALYSIS

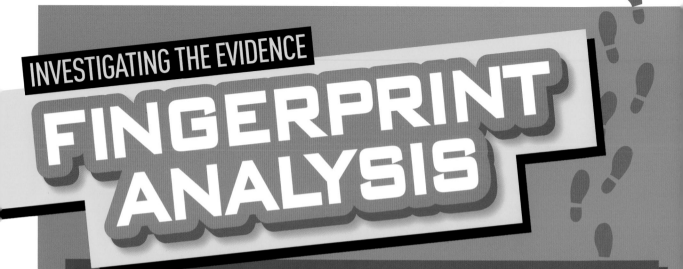

THERE WAS NO BLOOD EVIDENCE ON REDWOOD'S COMPUTER KEYBOARD, BUT PERHAPS THERE WERE STILL FINGERPRINTS LEFT BEHIND. Your next stop is the fingerprint lab. You bring the crowbar from the Dumpster along, too, in case it was used at the crime scene and there are prints to link it to a culprit.

ALTERNATIVE LIGHT SOURCE (ALS)

Before you dust for fingerprints, you'll want to know where you're most likely to find useful prints, so the first tool you'll need is an alternative light source, or ALS. You'll need to turn down the regular light in the lab and use the reflected ultraviolet imaging system, or RUVIS for short. The RUVIS looks like a long camera lens. You check the crowbar first, but there are no visible prints to be found. Unfortunately, it's possible that the thief was wearing gloves.

FIND THE BEST EVIDENCE

The keyboard is another story.

» When you turn on the RUVIS, it shines ultraviolet light onto the keys, and wherever there are good fingerprints, that UV light is reflected, making the prints much easier to see. UV light is usually invisible to our eyes, but the RUVIS converts it to light that we can see, and that's how you'll find the best evidence.

» When you shine the RUVIS on the keyboard, you see lots and lots of prints. Many are overlapping, and those can't be seen clearly enough to match, but there are two keys— the 8 key and the CONTROL key—with just one clean print each. You decide to focus on those.

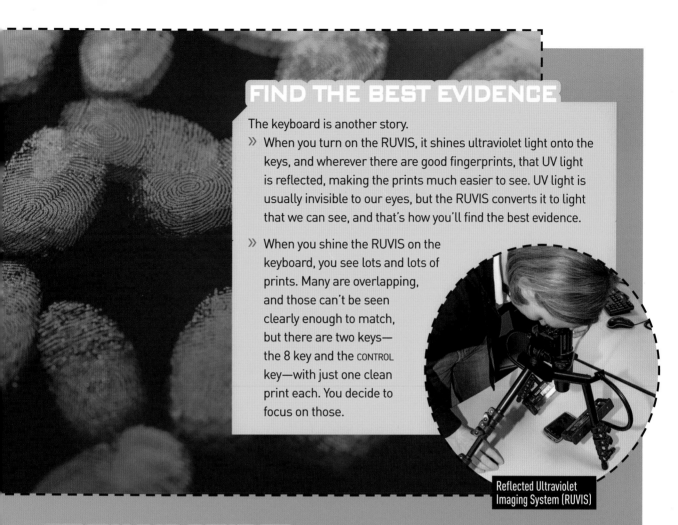

Reflected Ultraviolet
Imaging System (RUVIS)

REVEALING POWDER

The computer keys are black, so you choose a container of gray powder to dust for the prints so they'll show up. You'll also need a roll of clear fingerprinting tape, some index cards, and a fingerprint dusting brush.

» You dip the brush into the gray powder and tap it on the edge of the container to get rid of any extra powder. Then you wave the brush over the two keys, lightly and carefully, so you're just barely touching the prints. You should see powder attached to the fingerprint but very little sticking to the surrounding area, almost as if the powder "knows" what it's supposed to reveal. That's because it is made of aluminum dust. Metal elements generally carry a positive static charge. Human skin oils and sweat—both of which are present on fingerprints—carry a negative charge. Opposite electrical charges attract one another, so the powder is naturally attracted to the print, and only the print.

PRESERVING

» Once the prints are highlighted with the gray powder, it's time to preserve them. They need to be saved so they'll be useful as evidence. That's where the tape comes in. You tear off a piece, about the length of your thumb, being careful not to get your own fingerprints on the tape as you work. (This can be tricky because it's stickier than regular tape! It has to be, in order to get the whole print without leaving anything behind.) You push the piece of tape gently onto one of the dusted prints and rub your fingernail over it to make sure it's on tightly. Then you catch the edge of the tape and quickly remove it from the key, the way you'd pull off a bandage to get it over with all at once. You press the lifting tape onto an index card and see your newly captured print. Then you repeat the process for the fingerprint on the other key.

» Now it's time to run the prints through AFIS, the Automated Fingerprint Identification System.

An example of lifting tape being used to collect a fingerprint

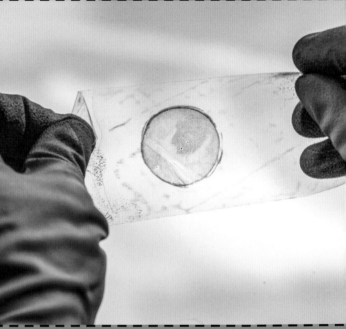

AUTOMATED FINGERPRINT IDENTIFICATION SYSTEM (AFIS)

Uses digital imaging to collect, store, and analyze fingerprints.

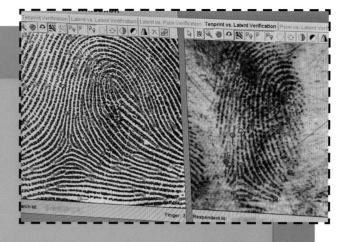

SCAN AND ANALYZE

» You start by placing the index cards on a scanner. You lower the cover, press SCAN, and follow the directions on the computer screen. Once the scanning process begins, you'll see your collected print appear on the left side of the screen while potential matches from the AFIS database whiz by on the right side. The computer scans fingerprints for ridge characteristics. If you look closely at your fingertips under a bright light, you might be able to see some of these tiny details, like curving lines, crosses, or *y* shapes. These create the differences in fingerprints from one person to another. With the AFIS system, prints need to be the same in a minimum of 16 spots to call it a match, and with a good print there are usually more than that.

» Finally, the AFIS scan slows down and settles on one print. The left and right sides of the computer screen each show a print with at least 30 numbered matching areas in common. You have a match! That means the print you collected from the crime scene is most likely from the person who supplied that print in the database. So whose print is it? You squint to read the identity on the AFIS screen ...

✷ AND THE RESULTS SHOW ... ✷

CHET REDWOOD. HE'S IN THE DATABASE BECAUSE IN ADDITION TO PEOPLE WHO ARE ARRESTED, AFIS HAS PRINTS FROM PEOPLE WHO ARE FINGERPRINTED FOR OTHER REASONS. IN MANY PLACES, EDUCATORS ARE FINGER-PRINTED AS A REQUIREMENT FOR EMPLOYMENT, IN ORDER TO KEEP STUDENTS SAFE.

Well, that match is no surprise. It's Redwood's computer, after all. But maybe the other print will reveal a suspect, so you start a new scan. Once again, you see your print on the left side of the screen and potential matches flashing by on the right. After a few minutes, AFIS signals a match for this print, too. This time, there are only about 20 matching areas, but that's still greater than the minimum of 16. The identity at the bottom says this print is a match for Dr. Jarrett Washington—Redwood's supervisor. Again, the match is no big surprise. It's possible that Washington was stealing information from Redwood's files, but it's also not unusual for a supervisor to use a staff member's computer.

DR. JARRETT WASHINGTON,
Redwood's supervisor

✷ It'll take more crime science to pin down your suspect. ✷

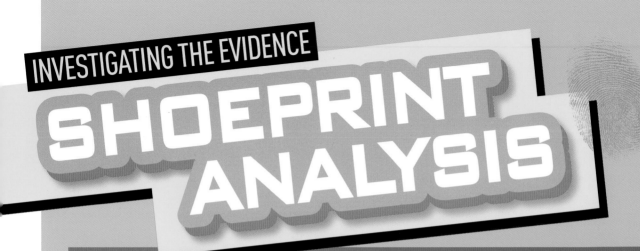

SHOEPRINT ANALYSIS

>> **THE MUDDY SHOEPRINTS FOUND OUTSIDE THE GREENHOUSE ARE A SOLID LEAD, SO YOUR NEXT JOB IS ANALYZING THOSE.** You stop at the crime lab to pick up a duffel bag full of supplies that includes a camera, a bottle of water, a bag of dental stone powder, a can of hair spray, a mixing spoon, and a casting frame, which is a rectangular frame that you'll put around the print on the ground to keep the poured plaster from running all over the place. Then you head back to the crime scene to make a plaster cast of your print.

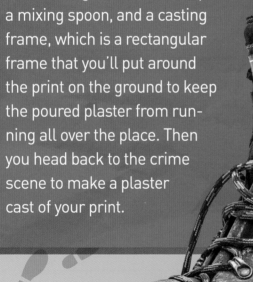

OBSERVE & RECORD

While there are several prints outside the greenhouse door, one is complete and cleaner than the rest, so you choose that one for your analysis. First, you photograph the print from directly above. You use a flashlight to illuminate different parts of the print.

PREP YOUR PLASTER & MOLD

A shoeprint specialist mixing water with stone powder

» Then you mix the plaster by pouring the bottle of water into the bag of dental stone powder. That's the same material they use to make dental impressions at the orthodontist, but in this case, you'll use it to make a model of a shoeprint instead of teeth.

» Once the water is poured in, you seal the bag, squeeze the bottom, and tip the whole thing back and forth to mix the water and powder. The mixture starts to look and feel a little like pancake batter.

» Next, you spray hair spray lightly all over the inside of the shoeprint impression. That hardens the print so the casting compound doesn't damage or change it. Then, you put the casting frame around the shoeprint to keep the plaster in place.

Pouring plaster into a print

MAKE THE CAST

Now it's time to make the cast.

» You open the bag of plaster and make a spout for pouring. Slowly and carefully, you pour the plaster into the print. It's important to take your time, so the wet plaster doesn't gush into the print too quickly and mess up the details!

» Once you've poured all the plaster into the print, you'll need to wait about 30 minutes for it to dry completely. As it hardens, you scratch identifying information into the drying cast—your initials, the date, and the words "greenhouse print."

» After about 30 minutes, your print should be dry enough to collect. You pry it up from the earth, and you put it in an evidence bag to return to the lab.

A dried plaster of a shoeprint

SCAN & ANALYZE

Once you get back to the lab, you lightly brush the dirt and debris from the cast. Then you start up the computer and open the shoeprint database. It's a database designed to search known and unknown footwear files so you can determine what kind of shoe made the print. Just enter the measurements of the print and an image, and the database will tell you information about the shoe.

Using a small tape measure, you discover that the impression on your cast measures 12¾ inches (32.4 cm) long, and it is 4½ inches (11.4 cm) wide at the ball of the foot. You enter that information, and then the computer program prompts you to upload an image. Using your camera, you take a photo from directly above the plaster cast and upload the image. It works a lot like the fingerprint database; the image of your greenhouse print appears on the left side of the screen while images of different shoeprints fly past on the right.

✱ AND THE RESULTS SHOW … ✱

UNFORTUNATELY, THE DATABASE DOESN'T COME BACK WITH A MATCH TO ANY PREVIOUSLY ENTERED SHOEPRINTS. IT DOES OFFER SOME INFORMATION, THOUGH— YOUR CAST IS FROM A SIZE 11½ MEN'S HIKING BOOT.

Both Sven Linnaeus and Finn Jamison wear this size shoe, so that's not enough information for you to close in on a suspect.

SVEN LINNAEUS, another university botany professor

FINN JAMISON, a botany student minoring in computer science

✱ But there's still more evidence from the greenhouse to be studied. ✱

PAINT ANALYSIS

>>> **THE CROWBAR FROM THE DUMPSTER DIDN'T HAVE ANY FINGERPRINTS TO ANALYZE, BUT IT DOES HAVE SOME GREEN AND WHITE PAINT SMUDGES.** They might help show if this was the tool that was used to break into the greenhouse. You've also brought a white paint sample from the greenhouse door's wood frame so the two can be compared.

INFRARED SPECTROSCOPY

To analyze your paint samples, you make use of a process called infrared spectroscopy. You'll use a special instrument called an FTIR (Fourier transform infrared) spectrometer which will expose your paint samples to a kind of intense light called infrared light.

FTIR spectrometer

WHAT IS INFRARED LIGHT?

It's different from the light we see with our eyes. That light is called visible light and includes all the colors of the rainbow—a whole spectrum of colors. Infrared light is a higher-energy light that our eyes can't see.

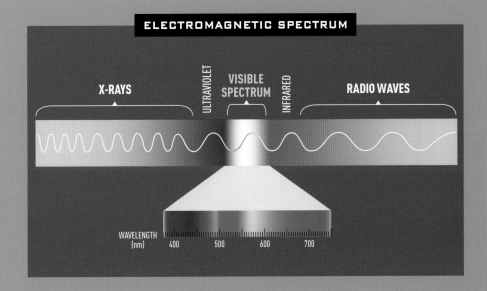

ELECTROMAGNETIC SPECTRUM

X-RAYS

ULTRAVIOLET

VISIBLE SPECTRUM

INFRARED

RADIO WAVES

WAVELENGTH (nm) 400 500 600 700

When the FTIR spectrometer exposes a paint sample to that infrared light, the infrared light shares some of its energy with the paint molecules, and those molecules then behave in different ways. Some of the light is absorbed by the paint, and some is reflected back. The compounds that make up the paint stretch, vibrate, and compress in unique ways, and the FTIR spectrometer captures this interaction between the paint and the infrared light.

That interaction is captured as a graph, which is unique to each substance—a sort of molecular fingerprint. And just as human fingerprints are unique, no two substances' graphs are exactly the same. The graph is then compared to the graphs of known substances. Sometimes, this information can trace a paint right back to its manufacturer, but for now, all you really want to know is whether the paint from the crowbar matches the paint from the greenhouse door.

✳ AND THE RESULTS SHOW … ✳

IT'S A MATCH! THE CROWBAR FOUND IN THE DUMPSTER OUTSIDE SVEN LINNAEUS'S OFFICE WAS INDEED THE TOOL USED TO BREAK INTO THE GREENHOUSE.

✳ Without fingerprints or other evidence, though, there's not enough information to accuse Linnaeus of committing the crime. ✳

A paint chip at high magnification

COMPUTER FORENSICS

>> **DID THE THIEF USE REDWOOD'S LAPTOP TO ACCESS INFORMATION ABOUT THE LOCATION OF THE STICKY WATTLE?** Fingerprints and strawberry jam smudges couldn't answer that question, but perhaps there are clues on the computer drive that will. Computer scientists can sometimes solve crimes by accessing the logs on a device to see if a computer has been broken into, or hacked.

SORT THROUGH

You start your analysis of Redwood's laptop by making a list of all the installed programs to see if anything appears suspicious. A program the computer's owner doesn't recognize or doesn't remember installing might be one that gave a hacker access to data. When you show your list to Redwood, he recognizes all the programs. Nothing suspicious there.

OUTSIDE INTRUSION

But sometimes, looking at things a different way can help shine a light on clues. So you sort the list of files another way—by date installed instead of alphabetically by file name. This time, when you share the list with Redwood, you ask if he's installed any new programs on his computer in the last couple of weeks. He says he hasn't, and now he notices a program on the laptop called BioBot. It was installed eight days ago. Could that be the software that allowed the hacker to see the files on his laptop and access information that was used to steal the rare plant? When you take a look at the log files on Redwood's laptop, you find multiple instances of a foreign IP address attempting to log in, and then opening and transferring files. In this case, "foreign" doesn't mean from another country; it just means that someone has been accessing the computer from a different location.

WHAT'S AN IP ADDRESS?

An IP address is a series of numbers and decimal points linked to all of the online activity on a computer. The numbers can range from 0.0.0.0 to 255.255.255.255, and they show where and how a computer is connecting to the internet. For example, if you go online at home, your home network or router will assign an IP address to your computer. If you take your computer to school or to a café, it will be assigned a different IP address when you connect from that location. IP addresses are unique; they're like the fingerprints of the computer world. So if you can find the source of the foreign IP address on the screen, then you may well have found your hacker and your thief.

✷ AND THE RESULTS SHOW … ✷

IT LOOKS LIKE REDWOOD'S HACKER MAY NOT BE EXPERIENCED. SO LOOKING UP THE IP ADDRESS MIGHT HELP POINT YOU TO THE PERSON WHO COMMITTED THE CRIME (OR AT LEAST THE COMPUTER THEY USED). THERE ARE SEVERAL WEBSITES WHERE YOU CAN LOOK UP IP ADDRESSES TO FIND OUT WHERE THE COMPUTER IS LOCATED.

You open one of those and enter the numbers, and it turns out the IP address of the hacker is local, from the same town where the university is located. The website doesn't give an exact physical location, though. For that, you'll need to contact the internet service provider, which will only release the information if you have a special order from a judge. You're actually pretty lucky to have discovered this digital fingerprint. Most experienced hackers know enough to clear the logs—covering those footprints so they don't leave such an obvious trace of what they've done and where they've been.

✷ Let's gather everything we know so far. ✷

LET'S REVIEW

HERE'S ANOTHER LOOK AT YOUR SUSPECTS, ALONG WITH THE EVIDENCE AND OTHER INFORMATION GATHERED SO FAR. **TAKE A FEW MINUTES TO REVIEW, AND THEN SEE IF YOU CAN DETERMINE WHO THE CULPRIT IS!**

UNIVERSITY GREENHOUSE

MAVIS LONGO,
a visiting pharmaceutical company researcher

MOTIVE: Money

Longo has a clear motive. Her attempt to purchase the plant for her company's research is evidence of that. But there's no physical evidence to connect her to the crime.

FINN JAMISON,
a botany student minoring in computer science

MOTIVE: Prestige

Jamison's motive is less clear, but it's possible he could have stolen the plant to pass off as his own discovery, or to donate to the botanical garden where he works. He also wears the same size shoe as that hiking boot that left the impression in the mud, and with his computer science background, there's a good chance he'd know the basics of hacking into a computer.

MOTIVE: Jealousy

It's possible that Linnaeus stole the plant because he was jealous of Redwood's accomplishments. There are no fingerprints to connect him to the crime scene, but he does wear the same shoe size as the hiking boot that left the print in the mud outside the greenhouse, and his office is close to the Dumpster where the muddy gloves and crowbar were found.

SVEN LINNAEUS,
another university botany professor

DR. JARRETT WASHINGTON,
Redwood's supervisor

MOTIVE: Job security

Washington had a possible motive for committing the crime—to secure his status at the university. And his fingerprints were found on Redwood's laptop. He wears a smaller shoe size than the hiking boot that left the print, but might he have worn larger shoes that day to make it look like someone with bigger feet committed the crime?

✲ Who do you think DID IT?
Turn the page to find out! ✲

THE SOLUTION

AND THE CULPRITS ARE ...

☹ FINN JAMISON!

MAVIS LONGO!

Based on the information you gathered from the forensic analysis of finger-prints, paint chips, and shoeprints, along with your computer forensics results, a judge issues an order for the internet service provider to release the details of the IP address from the computer that hacked Redwood's laptop. You expect that it will most likely be traced to Sven Linnaeus, Redwood's scientific rival whose office was near the Dumpster where the muddy gloves and crowbar were found.

SOLVED

INSTEAD, IT'S TRACED TO A COMPUTER AT 27 MAPLE STREET. THAT'S FINN JAMISON'S APARTMENT!

When police arrive with a warrant giving them permission to search his home, they find not only the missing plant but also a pair of muddy, size 11½ hiking boots shoved into the back of a closet. Finn Jamison's computer science background provided him with the basic skills to hack into Redwood's laptop, where Jamison learned where the plant was being kept. Jamison also downloaded Redwood's research files. He used the crowbar to pry open the greenhouse door, stole the plant, and then tossed his gloves and crowbar into the Dumpster outside Linnaeus's office to make it appear that Linnaeus was the culprit. Confronted with the evidence against him, Jamison confessed that he'd stolen the plant and had made arrangements to sell it to Mavis Longo's pharmaceutical company, along with Redwood's valuable research files. Police arrested both Jamison and Longo, thanks to the help of crime-solving science.

A CLOSER LOOK

FINGERPRINTING

>>> **THE USE OF FINGERPRINTING TO IDENTIFY A PERSON GOES BACK HUNDREDS OF YEARS. IN THE 700S, THE CHINESE USED INK-ON-PAPER FINGERPRINTS FOR BUSINESS TRANSACTIONS.** Ancient Babylonians did this, too, pressing their fingertips into clay to seal a deal. But it wasn't until the late 1800s that investigators realized fingerprints could help solve crimes.

HENRY FAULDS

In the late 1870s, an English doctor named Henry Faulds was involved in an archaeological dig in Japan when he found fingerprints that artists had left in the clay of their pottery. It made him curious about how prints could be used to identify a person, so he started studying modern people's fingerprints. In 1880, Faulds published his ideas in a scientific magazine, suggesting that fingerprints might be useful in catching criminals.

FRANCIS GALTON

While he was studying fingerprints, Faulds wrote to his cousin, the famous naturalist Charles Darwin, to share his ideas and ask for help creating a system to classify them. Darwin was busy with other studies, but he sent the letter along to his half cousin, Francis Galton, who ended up collecting more than 8,000 prints. In 1892, Galton wrote a book called *Finger Prints,* outlining a system to classify prints based on patterns of arches, loops, and whorls. By the early 1900s, the technique was being used by law enforcement in both Britain and the United States.

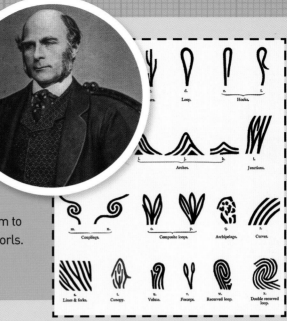

Real-World CRIME SCIENCE!

Fingerprints were first used as evidence in a criminal trial in the United States in 1910. After a murder in Chicago, police found a fingerprint on a recently painted railing at the victim's house. The suspect, a man named Thomas Jennings, already had a criminal record, and his prints matched the one left on the railing. Jennings was found guilty of the crime. This was the first time that a court determined that fingerprints were, in fact, a reliable method for identification.

Fingerprint evidence also helped to convict a notorious American gang member. In 1933, George "Machine Gun" Kelly and another man had kidnapped a wealthy man named Charles Urschel and demanded ransom. After he was kidnapped, Urschel made it a point to leave his fingerprints on anything he could touch at the home where he was being held. Those fingerprints, found at a farm owned by Kelly's father-in-law, became important evidence in the trial.

George Kelly

Sometimes, fingerprints can be used to solve crimes that happened a long time ago. In 2008, police in Nebraska got a tip about a 1978 case they'd been unable to solve at the time. They'd collected fingerprints from the crime scene, but the FBI's national fingerprint database wasn't fully up and running in 1978. But when police reopened the case thirty years later, they were able to run the prints through the database and come up with a match. It led to the arrest of a man who was already serving time in prison for a burglary. Finally, the old cold case was solved!

DUSTING FOR FINGERPRINTS

Fingerprint-lifting powders can consist of anything from finely ground metals to carbon powder to ... cinnamon! Crime scene investigators use lifting powders to expose the prints on a surface. Then they "lift" the prints with clear tape and tape those lifted prints onto a white card, which becomes a permanent piece of evidence. Not surprisingly, lifting powders and tapes work best on smooth, nonporous surfaces. Porous surfaces like fabrics have tiny holes that air and liquid can pass through, so it's harder to see fingerprints on those. But the oil from people's fingers will remain and be a lot clearer on nonporous surfaces like glass.

>> WHAT YOU'LL NEED

- 1 tablespoon (15 g) of finely ground cinnamon
- A small, shallow bowl
- A smooth, hard surface
- A clean, dry makeup brush with long, soft bristles
- Clear sticky tape
- A white index card
- Cooking spray (optional)

✷ Ready to try your hand at lifting fingerprints? ✷

>> PROCEDURE

1   Put the cinnamon into the bowl.

2   Rub one of your fingers on your forehead, along your nose, and behind your ear to get plenty of skin oils on it. If you are not a particularly oily-skinned person, you can spray your finger with a little cooking spray and blot it on a paper towel.

3   Make a fingerprint by pressing your finger down on a **smooth,** hard surface. **Clean** glass and **smooth** countertops work great. Be sure to remember where you left the print!

4   Dip the ends of the makeup brush bristles into the cinnamon. Tap the handle of the brush on the edge of the bowl to remove excess cinnamon.

5   Gently wave the makeup brush over your finger-print in a circle, touching just the very tips of the bristles to the print, until the print shows up in a brown color.

6   Cut off a piece of clear tape long enough to cover the fingerprint and carefully lay it right onto the fingerprint, sticky side down.

7   Rub the tape onto the print with the flat side of your fingernail to get all the air bubbles out. Then, carefully lift the tape off the surface. Most or all of your fingerprint should now be on the tape!

8   Stick the tape onto your index card. See if you can tell what kind of print you have! Is it a loop, a whorl, or an arch?

>> HOW IT WORKS

Lifting powders have an overall positive electrical charge. Oils have a negative charge. Opposite charges attract, and that's why lifting powders seem to stick to the oily print.

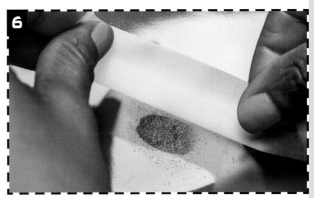

FINGERPRINT PATTERNS

LOOP   WHORL   ARCH

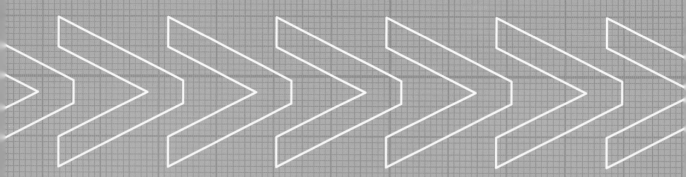

BONOBO RANSOM

MISSING

SCENARIO

SITUATION NOTES:

Someone broke into the primate exhibit at the zoo overnight and kidnapped Bombo, a young bonobo. Born just a year ago, Bombo has been the zoo's most popular resident, leading to record crowds. Chimp caretaker Lucy Matthews discovered the missing bonobo when she arrived to feed the animals before the zoo opened for the day. She reported the incident to zoo director May Wilson.

DO NOT CROSS

CROSS   DO NOT CROSS   DO NOT CROSS   DO NOT CROS

⟫ RANSOM NOTE

1

Sometimes, kidnappers leave behind a ransom note, demanding money for the safe return of the person (or bonobo!) who was kidnapped. Sure enough, caretaker Lucy Matthews said she found a note like that on the floor of the bonobo house. It's hand-written in black pen on a piece of plain white paper.

To Whom it may concern,
I have taken Bombo. He is safe and will be well cared for while he is gone. To get him back, you must pay a ransom of $10,000. Put cash in an unmarked suitcase and leave it by the monkey bars at Oak Street Park at 10 p.m. on Friday night.

DO NOT CROSS
DO NOT CROSS
DO NOT CROSS
DO NOT CROSS

GROGGY ADULT BONOBOS

2 Bombo's parents, Moby and Koko, weren't kidnapped along with their baby. But they're strangely groggy, as if they've been sedated.

DOOR TO THE BONOBO HOUSE

3

There are no broken windows on the bonobo house, so whoever stole Bombo must have come in through the main door. The door isn't damaged, but perhaps there will be fingerprints or other evidence left behind on it.

4

VIALS OF BLOOD

Zookeepers worry about health concerns any time an animal is acting strangely. In this case, given how sleepy Moby and Koko are acting, it might be a good idea to draw some blood for testing.

THE SUSPECTS

WHAT KIND OF PERSON WOULD STEAL A BABY BONOBO? AFTER INTERVIEWING CHIMP CARETAKER LUCY MATTHEWS AND ZOO DIRECTOR MAY WILSON, DETECTIVES CAME UP WITH THE FOLLOWING LIST OF SUSPECTS:

OSCAR MULVANEY,
a former overnight security guard at the zoo

MOTIVE: Revenge

Mulvaney was fired two months ago after the zoo director, May Wilson, discovered he'd been sleeping on the job. His last words before leaving were "You'll be sorry!" Wilson says Mulvaney would have known the layout of the zoo as well as the schedule for the security shift changes.

BURT BRASHER,
director of the nearby Wild Animal
Safari Experience

MOTIVE: Money

Brasher's wild animal safari center used to be busy every day of the year, but recently, the zoo has become more popular, and Brasher has struggled to pay his bills.

MOTIVE: Money

Wong worked closely with Matthews, and when the two talked, she expressed frustration that the cost of her college tuition had gone up again. She'd taken a part-time job at the Wild Animal Safari Experience to earn some money but didn't think it would be enough. Wong was familiar with the primate exhibit layout and would have been able to approach the animals at night without causing alarm.

MIA WONG,
a college intern whose volunteer
work at the zoo just wrapped up

MOTIVE: Sabotage

Armstrong and Wilson were fierce rivals in college. Armstrong, who works at the zoo, had applied to be its director but Wilson got the job.

ZORA ARMSTRONG,
a zoologist who went to college with
zoo director May Wilson

TOXICOLOGY

>> **BY THE TIME YOU GET TO THE ZOO TO INVESTIGATE, THE ADULT BONOBOS ARE HAVING BREAKFAST,** but caretaker Lucy Matthews tells you that they were nearly nonresponsive when she first arrived that morning. She believes they must have been drugged so that the baby bonobo could be taken from the enclosure.

Bonobos are powerful creatures. Anyone who knows that would understand that stealing a baby would be difficult, if not impossible, unless the adult bonobos were sedated. You ask Matthews to draw blood from the bonobos so that you can take the samples to the toxicology lab to find out what happened.

BONOBO

WHAT IS TOXICOLOGY?

Toxicology is a branch of science that involves the study of chemicals and their negative effects on living things. Toxicology is used in forensics to identify drugs or other substances that were involved in a crime.

GATHERING SAMPLES

Once the blood is drawn, the vials are packed and transported to the toxicology lab. Because the bonobos were still drowsy when Matthews arrived at the zoo, she guessed that they'd been drugged with some kind of sedative—a drug that has a calming effect and can cause sleep. In order to prove that, you'll need to positively identify any foreign substances in the chimps' blood—anything that wouldn't naturally be there, like drugs.

To begin that discovery process, a tech runs the samples through an instrument called GC-MS, a gas chromatograph–mass spectrometer.

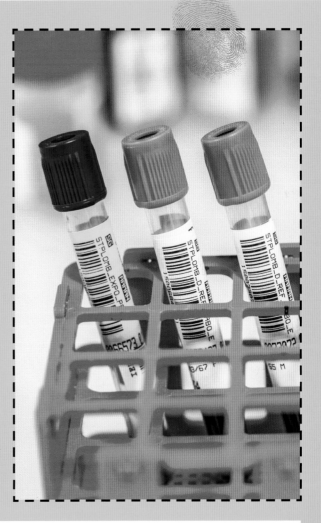

GAS CHROMATOGRAPH-MASS SPECTROMETER

The GC-MS looks like two large, rectangular copy machines connected by a tube. It has an injection area on one side and a detector on the other. Its job is to separate a sample into its individual chemical parts.

In this case, it will separate the bonobos' blood from any foreign substances, like one that might have put them to sleep. You'll be looking for traces of a group of chemicals that are commonly used as a sedative to calm aggressive animals or to put animals to sleep before surgery. You program the computer to match your unknown substance to known animal sedatives.

It's time to see if your blood sample brings up a match.

A scientist places a vial of fluid into a GC-MS.

SEPARATE & ANALYZE

» Using a centrifuge, a fast-spinning container that separates fluids of different densities, the blood is separated into cells and a liquid portion, which would include any foreign chemicals.

» The tech injects that liquid into the injection port of the GC-MS to begin the process. As the sample travels through the column of the heated oven inside the instrument, it's separated into the parts of the mixture. At the end of the first machine, called a gas chromatograph, the sample comes out separated into its parts. Next, it goes through the tube to the second machine, called a mass spectrometer.

SEPARATED BLOOD

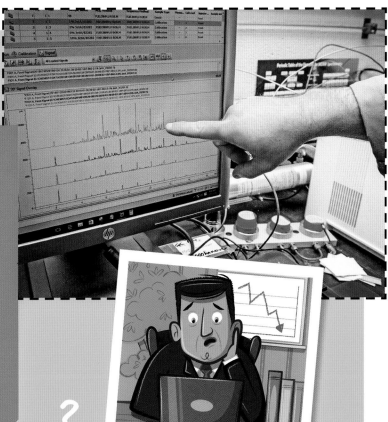

» In the mass spectrometer, your sample goes through a process that breaks it down even more, into all of its different chemical components. The instrument creates a graph of all the different parts, and that graph is then compared to the graphs of known substances.

When the chromatogram from your first sample is complete, it shows matches to several known sedatives. They're commonly used in combination to allow a veterinarian to approach animals that may otherwise be uncooperative. You run a blood sample from the second bonobo parent through the GC-MS and get the same results.

BURT BRASHER, director of the nearby Wild Animal Safari Experience

☆ AND THE RESULTS SHOW … ☆

… YOUR SUSPICIONS ARE RIGHT! SOMEONE DID DRUG BOTH OF THE BABY BONOBO'S PARENTS. THE QUESTION NOW IS WHO?

Two of your four suspects—Brasher and Armstrong—work directly with animals in zoo environments and would have had access to drugs and the knowledge to use sedatives like those found in the toxicology results. Wong, who was an intern, wouldn't have had access. And it's unlikely that Mulvaney would have had this experience as a security guard, but on his nightly rounds, he might have gained access to the labs where the drugs are kept.

ZORA ARMSTRONG, a zoologist who went to college with zoo director May Wilson

☆ You'll need to do some more investigating to narrow down your list of suspects. ☆

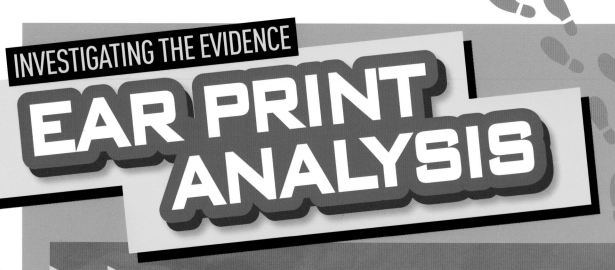

EAR PRINT ANALYSIS

WHEN YOU CHECK FOR FINGERPRINTS ON THE DOOR HANDLE TO THE BONOBO HOUSE, YOU DON'T FIND ANY. Most likely, whoever committed this crime was smart enough to wear gloves to cover their hands. But did they think to cover their ears?

It's likely that whoever broke into the bonobo house waited until the adult bonobos, at least, were asleep. Might they have listened at a window or door to make sure it was quiet inside before entering? If they did, they might have left behind an ear print.

EAR PRINTS

Ear prints are like fingerprints in that they can help to determine if a person was at the scene of a crime. When a person presses their ear up to a door or window to listen, wax and oils on their ear may be left behind on that surface. And like fingerprints, ear prints have unique characteristics, or points, that can be analyzed. Even if an ear print doesn't match a known print from a database, it might be useful in ruling out suspects who were around the crime scene.

COLLECT & SCAN

To check for ear prints around the bonobo house, you'll use dusting powder, just like you'd use in a search for fingerprints.

» You start with the door to the bonobo house, and sure enough, as you spread the dust, a fairly clear ear print appears. You can see where someone pressed their ear to the right side of the door.

» Using the same procedure you use for collecting fingerprints, you save the print by pressing a piece of tape over it so that the dusted print is transferred to the tape and then to a card.

» You return to the lab with the print and scan it so it can be compared to others in the ear print database.

EXAMPLE EAR PRINT

* AND THE RESULTS SHOW ... *

UNFORTUNATELY, IT DOESN'T COME BACK WITH A MATCH. YOU'RE DISAPPOINTED BUT NOT SURPRISED.

Ear prints aren't used as commonly as fingerprints are in criminal investigations, and the database of known ear prints is a lot smaller.

But finding and collecting this print wasn't a waste of time. Its location alone might provide you with a clue about who left it. The print was found high up on the door, almost six feet (1.82 m) off the ground. It's possible the suspect was standing on something as they listened, but more likely than not, your bonobo kidnapper is fairly tall. Unfortunately, that describes most of your suspects. With the exception of Mia Wong, who's five feet six inches tall (1.68 m), they're all at least six feet tall.

If your suspects are willing, you can also collect prints from their ears. This can be done either digitally, with a special 3D camera, or with a special kind of plastic that's rolled from the bottom of a suspect's ear to the top. Zora Armstrong and Burt Brasher are unavailable, but Oscar Mulvaney agrees to have his ear print taken. Based on what you can see, it doesn't appear to be a match with the print from the door.

MIA WONG,
a college intern whose volunteer work at the zoo just wrapped up

EAR PRINTS CAN VARY, THOUGH, BASED ON HOW HARD SOMEONE PRESSES THEIR EAR AGAINST A SURFACE. SO MULVANEY CAN'T BE RULED OUT AS A SUSPECT JUST YET.

* For now, you'll need to check out some other evidence. *

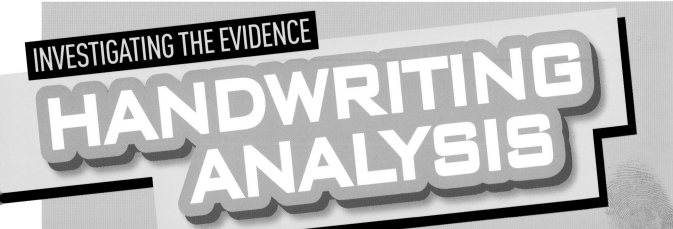

HANDWRITING ANALYSIS

CARETAKER LUCY MATTHEWS SHOWS YOU THE PAPER SHE FOUND ON THE FLOOR OF THE BONOBO HOUSE RIGHT AFTER SHE REALIZED THAT BOMBO WAS GONE. She'd picked it up before realizing it was a ransom note. The note is obviously an important clue, so you collect it, take photographs so that the handwriting can be analyzed, and place the note in an evidence bag.

While handwriting analysis is not really a science, it can still be used to point toward a suspect or cast doubt on one.

The letters of greatest interest are more complicated letters like j, t, q, g, and e, since they show the most differences from person to person.

66

To Whom it may concern:
I have taken Bombo. He is safe and will be well cared for while he is gone. To get him back, you must pay a ransom of $10,000. Put cash in an unmarked suitcase and leave it by the monkey bars at Oak Street Park at 10 p.m. on Friday night.

September 14, 4:30pm—
Giraffe feeding with kids
from school group.

Checked on polar bears
before leaving. Snowball
active but Elsa seemed
sluggish. Will check in with
her first thing tomorrow.

ZORA ARMSTRONG'S WORK JOURNAL

GATHER YOUR SAMPLES

You deliver the ransom note to a handwriting-analysis expert, who explains that she'll also need a sample of each suspect's handwriting, if possible. The trick is to get a suspect to leave a sample of their writing (also called an exemplar) without realizing it is being used for evidence; it's common for a suspect under observation to attempt to disguise their writing. In addition, it is wise to get the suspect to write similar words to those found in the ransom note or forged document.

The story of the baby bonobo kidnapping has already been on the morning news, so it's likely that all of your suspects already know that police are investigating the crime. It would be difficult to get valid handwriting samples now.

However, you're in luck because three of your four suspects—Oscar Mulvaney, Mia Wong, and Zora Armstrong—worked at the zoo. That means they took notes in their daily journals or wrote in employee logs. Burt Brasher never worked at the zoo, but he did write to zoo director May Wilson a few years ago, asking her to review a book he'd written about elephants. And you're in luck! Wilson still has the letter. She kept it because she thought Brasher's elephant stationery was cute and had meant to order some for herself. You make a quick trip back to the zoo to pick up all of the handwriting samples and bring them back to the lab.

July 1, 10:15 a.m.—
Morning feeding of emperor penguins.
Presentation for summer camp field trip.
So many questions!

Dear Dr. Wilson,
    I am writing to request that you review an upcoming book, Elephant Extravaganza, which explores the natural history and life of African Elephants.
Please read the enclosed sample of my book and send your recommendation to my publicist, Kiki Starr, no later than Friday, October 5.

Many thanks,
Burt Brasher
Author and Director of Wildlife Animal Safari Experience

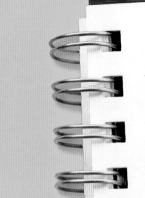

April 2—

11:30 p.m.— All quiet

12:30 p.m.—Disturbance near elephant enclosure outside main fence— youths with firecrackers, called city police to investigate.

1:30 a.m.—All quiet.

ANALYZE

Working with the handwriting-analysis expert, you study the ransom note side by side with each of your suspects' handwriting samples.

OSCAR MULVANEY'S SECURITY LOG

Mulvaney's security log is printed rather than written in cursive, so it's hard to tell if his writing might be similar.

11:30 p.m. — All quiet

12:30 p.m. — Disturbance near elephant enclosure outside main fence — youths with firecrackers, called city police to investigate.

1:30 a.m. — All quiet.

April 2 —

11:30 p.m. — All quiet

12:30 p.m. — Disturbance elephant enclosure out fence — youths wit kers, called city vestigate. quiet.

MIA WONG'S WORK JOURNAL

Mia Wong's handwriting is much neater than the writing in the ransom note, and there are no similarities in how letters are made.

July 1, 10:15 a.m. —
Morning feeding of penguins.
Presentation for summer field trip.
So many questions

July 1, 10:15 a.m. —
Morning feeding of emperor penguins.
Presentation for summer camp field trip.
So many questions!

September 14, 4:30pm — Giraffe feeding with kid from school group.

Checked on polar before leaving. active but Elsa sluggish. Will her first thin

September 14, 4:30 Giraffe feeding with k from school group.

Checked on polar bears before leaving. Snow bal active but Elsa seemed sluggish. Will check in or first thing tomor

ZORA ARMSTRONG'S WORK JOURNAL

Armstrong's writing is a mix of cursive and print, and it doesn't seem to match either.

Dear Dr. Wilson,
I am writi...
request that
an upcomin
Elephant E
which e
natural
of Afric

BURT BRASHER'S LETTER

There are definitely some similarities between the ransom note and Burt Brasher's handwriting in his letter to May Wilson.

Brasher makes big loops on his lowercase *g* and *j*, just like the writer of the ransom note. Brasher also crosses his lowercase *t* with an upward slant. However, there are also notable differences between the two samples, so this evidence is inconclusive. It's important to note that a person's handwriting can change over time.

BURT BRASHER,
director of the nearby Wild Animal Safari Experience

BUT THIS LETTER MIGHT ALSO OFFER SOMETHING THAT CAN'T CHANGE—FINGERPRINTS.

✱ You head to the fingerprint lab, hopeful that you might find the answers you've been searching for there. ✱

FINGERPRINT ANALYSIS

>> **EVEN THOUGH THERE WERE NO FINGERPRINTS FOUND ON ANY SURFACES IN THE BONOBO HOUSE, THIS RANSOM NOTE MAY BE ANOTHER STORY.**

Usually when we think of fingerprint analysis, we imagine detectives dusting for prints on hard surfaces like counters, doorknobs, and drinking glasses. But it's also possible to collect fingerprints from paper using a special process that involves using a chemical called ninhydrin.

NINHYDRIN

Ninhydrin is a chemical that reacts with substances left behind by human skin and the salts found in human sweat.

EXAMPLE OF PRINTS DEVELOPED WITH NINHYDRIN

COLLECT & SCAN

At the fingerprint lab, you find a spray bottle of ninhydrin.

» Wearing gloves, you spray the ransom note. Right away, several prints begin to emerge as detailed, dark purple fingerprints. Being careful not to smear the newly exposed but still wet fingerprints, you take several photographs of each print. The question now is, will they be a match for any prints that are already in AFIS.

» You upload your photos into the computer and wait for it to compare your prints to the prints in the database.

There's no match for your first set of prints. That's not surprising to you because you knew that Lucy had handled the ransom note. And she's never been accused of a crime or been fingerprinted for any other reason, so she's not in AFIS. But maybe it will be a different story for whoever left that second set of prints. You wait impatiently for the next result.

To Whom it may concern: I have taken Bombo. He is safe and will be well cared for while he is gone. ... back you ... pay a ransom ...000. Put cash in ...rked suitcase ...e it by the ...bars at Oak ...rk at 10p.m. on ...night.

★ AND THE TEST SHOWS ... ★

THIS ONE HAS A MATCH! WHEN IT COMES UP ON THE SCREEN, YOU SEE THE PRINT YOU SUBMITTED NEXT TO ONE PREVIOUSLY ENTERED INTO AFIS.

The computer shows all of the different matching details, called ridge characteristics, and it's a good match—there are more than 150 matching points on the prints! This person was in the AFIS system because of a previous arrest. The name next to the prints? Burtrand J. Brasher, arrested 15 years ago for breaking and entering and for a felony burglary charge.

THAT'S ENOUGH EVIDENCE FOR A JUDGE TO ISSUE A SEARCH WARRANT **FOR BURT BRASHER'S HOME AND THE WILD ANIMAL SAFARI EXPERIENCE OFFICES.**

BURT BRASHER, director of the nearby Wild Animal Safari Experience

★ Let's gather everything we know so far. ★

73

LET'S REVIEW

OSCAR MULVANEY,
a former overnight
security guard at the zoo

MOTIVE: Revenge

Mulvaney has a clear motive, since he'd been fired from the zoo and had promised to get revenge. He's the right height to have left the ear print on the door, but the ear print he provided didn't look the same, and his handwriting didn't match the writing on the ransom note.

MOTIVE: Money

Brasher's wild animal park has been struggling, so he had a motive to kidnap Bombo and ask for a ransom. As someone who works with animals, he would know how to care for Bombo and would have access to the kinds of drugs found in the adult bonobos' toxicology reports. He's also the right height to have left that ear print on the door, and his handwriting and fingerprints match those found on the ransom note.

BURT BRASHER,
director of the nearby Wild Animal Safari Experience

MOTIVE: Money

Wong had a motive to commit the crime—a need for money to pay her college tuition. But she's too short to have left the ear print unless she stood on something, and her handwriting looks nothing like the writing in the ransom note.

MIA WONG,
a college intern whose volunteer work at the zoo just wrapped up

ZORA ARMSTRONG,
a zoologist who went to college with zoo director May Wilson

MOTIVE: Sabotage

Armstrong had a possible motive to kidnap Bombo: her jealousy of zoo director May Wilson, who got the job Armstrong wanted. As a zoologist, she'd know how to care for Bombo, and she's tall enough to be the person who left the ear print. Her handwriting didn't seem like a very good match for the ransom note, though.

✶ Who do you think DID IT?
Turn the page to find out! ✶

THE SOLUTION

AND THE CULPRIT IS ...

☹ BURT BRASHER!

Once the search warrant was issued, you had all the evidence you needed. The medicines collected from Brasher's home included the two substances that showed up in the toxicology reports.

SOLVED

WHEN A JUDGE ORDERED BRASHER TO PROVIDE AN EAR PRINT, IT WAS A CLOSE MATCH WITH THE PRINT FOUND ON THE DOOR. Confronted with this evidence, as well as news that his handwriting was a match and that his fingerprints were identified on Bombo's ransom note, Brasher confessed to the crime. He led police to a shed on his property where they found Bombo unharmed. Brasher admitted that even though he'd left a ransom note, he had no intention of returning the kidnapped bonobo to the zoo. He had planned to keep Bombo hidden for a while and then announce later on that he'd acquired his own bonobo for the Wild Animal Safari Experience.

A CLOSER LOOK

HANDWRITING ANALYSIS

>>> **LIKE FINGERPRINTS, HANDWRITING IS ANOTHER KIND OF PERSONAL MARKER—EACH PERSON'S WRITING HAS SPECIFIC TRAITS THAT CAN SOMETIMES BE USED TO DETERMINE WHO WROTE A DOCUMENT.** People have understood for a long time that handwriting is unique. Way back in 500 B.C., the Chinese philosopher Confucius is said to have warned people, "Beware of a man whose writing sways like a reed in the wind."

Handwriting analysis, or graphology, actually began with the thought that you could tell a person's personality by their handwriting. An Italian doctor named Camillo Baldi published the first book about this in 1622. It was much later that people began analyzing handwriting and comparing samples to figure out who wrote something. In 1910, Albert Sherman Osborn wrote a book called *Questioned Documents*, all about how handwriting analysis can determine if a document is real or a fraud.

Real-World CRIME SCIENCE!

THE LINDBERGH KIDNAPPING

The most famous case that used handwriting analysis as evidence was the kidnapping of Charles Lindbergh, Jr. He was the son of pilot Charles Lindbergh, who was famous for making the first solo nonstop flight across the Atlantic. When the police first started investigating this case, they didn't have much evidence to work with. There were no fingerprints or bloodstains, and footprints in the mud outside the home were too messy to measure.

But investigators did end up with a dozen ransom notes, delivered in the month after the kidnapping. The police sent those notes to handwriting experts, who agreed that

they'd all been written by the same person. When the investigation led police to Bruno Richard Hauptmann, they sent samples of his handwriting to the FBI, where the exemplars were compared to the writing in the ransom notes. They matched, and this evidence was used at trial to help convict Hauptmann of the crime.

Bruno Richard Hauptmann

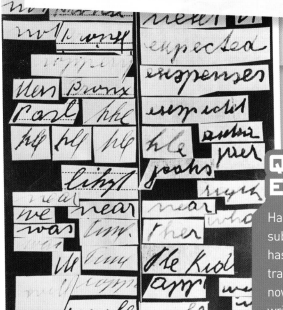

QUESTIONABLE EVIDENCE?

Handwriting analysis isn't a perfect science. It's subjective, a matter of the opinions of experts, so it hasn't always been widely accepted in courts. But the training of experts has improved over the years. And now, there are computerized databases for handwriting samples, just like there are for fingerprints and DNA. FISH (Forensic Information System for Handwriting) is maintained by the United States Secret Service Forensics Laboratory and contains tens of thousands of handwriting samples so investigators can scan in handwritten documents for comparison.

ANALYZING DOCUMENTS

Document analysis is a specialty area of crime scene investigation that involves techniques in fingerprinting, handwriting analysis, and ink chromatography. Using all three would give investigators a really good idea who created or altered a document like a ransom note, forged check, or forged celebrity signature.

>> WHAT YOU'LL NEED

- Four friends or family members
- Five pieces of white construction paper
- Four different brands of black markers
- Scissors
- Rubbing alcohol
- Five clean, dry drinking glasses (or jars)

✻ Are you ready to try your hand at this kind of analysis? ✻

>> PROCEDURE

1 Give one piece of construction paper to each friend or family member. Also give each one of them a different brand of black marker.

2 Show them the Bombo ransom note and have them copy it word for word in their own normal handwriting on the construction paper. Assign each person a number and label their papers at the top: Suspect 1, Suspect 2, Suspect 3, and Suspect 4.

3 Next, have them choose one of the four to be the official "culprit." You should leave the room while they do this, and make sure they don't tell you who the culprit is! While you're gone, that person needs to provide an exemplar handwriting sample for comparison. On the fifth piece of white construction paper with the same marker they used before and using their normal writing, the person designated as the culprit should write this sentence, which uses all the letters of the alphabet: The quick brown fox jumps over the lazy dog. When that's done, have your helpers label that paper "Exemplar" and then call you to return to the room.

4 Next, place all of the samples together with the exemplar and analyze the handwriting to see if you can begin to determine which ransom note was written by the same person who wrote the exemplar.

Pay close attention to the following:

- How letters slant: Do the letters slant forward? Backward? Do the lines of the sentences flow upward or downward?

- Complex letters like *g, j, q,* and *e*: Do they have big loops, small loops, or no loops?

- How the writers cross their *t*'s and dot their *i*'s.

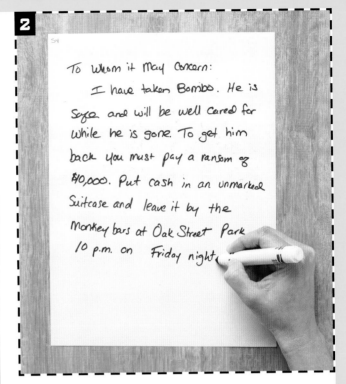

✱ Do you have a preliminary idea about who your suspect might be? Let's confirm with ink chromatography! ✱

7

8

>> PROCEDURE

5 Using both the suspect's exemplar and the four original handwriting samples, find an area of each construction paper sheet that has a little writing at one end but is mostly blank. Cut a strip from it about one inch (2.5 cm) wide and four inches long.

6 Pour just enough rubbing alcohol into each of the five glasses so the alcohol just covers the bottom of the glass. Label the top of each strip (where there is no ink) in pencil so you know which are the samples and which is the exemplar. You can use the initials of each: E for exemplar, S1 for your first suspect, S2 for the second, and so on.

7 Gently lower each strip into the alcohol. Make sure the ink ends just above the alcohol and that the blank area is toward the top of the glass. Carefully tape the top of each strip to the top of its jar.

8 Leave the strips in the alcohol for about 20 to 30 minutes or until you see the black ink separate into different colors. **Do not move or disturb** the strips during this time. Depending on the composition of the ink, you might see it separate from black into two, three, or even four different colors.

Pay close attention to the following:

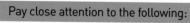

- How many colors did the ink on each strip separate into?

- What pattern did the ink make as it separated?

- Do two of the strips look more similar than the others?

9 Use the handwriting analysis and ink-separation chromatography to make your guess about which of your friends or family members provided the exemplar. Ask your suspects who was the culprit who wrote the exemplar to find out if you were right!

>> HOW IT WORKS

Black inks and paints are usually a mixture of multiple pigments, or colors. Those different colors are dissolved in a solvent, which is a liquid in which other substances dissolve. Each pigment is made of different chemical parts. Some of those pigments will dissolve more quickly than others, and some have stronger chemical attractions to the construction paper. Because of this, the pigments travel up the paper at different rates, separating into the different colors in the mixture.

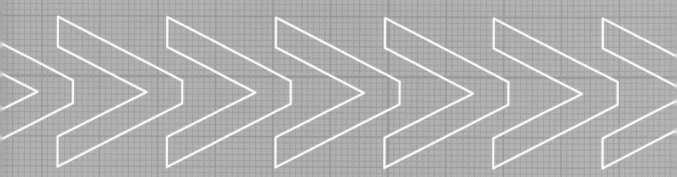

THE GRAVE ROBBER'S MISTAKE

MISSING

DO NOT CROSS DO NOT CROSS DO NOT CROSS DO NOT CROSS DO NOT CROSS ROSS DO NOT CROSS DO NOT CROSS DO NOT CROSS DO NOT CRO

SITUATION NOTES:

Every year, Yuna Okada visits the graves of her family members buried in the local cemetery. Her great-grandfather, Mori Okada, had been buried with a priceless treasure: a sword that had been in their family for generations. Yuna takes great pride in her family's history.

But this year, Yuna knew something was wrong as soon as she turned the corner in the cemetery and started along the path that led to the gravesite. Someone had disturbed her great-grandfather's final resting place, and the priceless sword was gone!

MORI OKADA
BORN
DECEMBER 1, 1870
DIED
MAY 3, 1953

THE EVIDENCE

>> DISTURBED GRAVE

1

Mori Okada's gravestone is pushed out of place, and the area around it is a muddy mess. Whoever did this tried to cover it up, but the grave has clearly been disturbed.

>> RED SMUDGE

There's a red smudge on the edge of the gravestone. Could it be blood?

2

>> MISSING SWORD

3

When cemetery caretaker Henry Sato is called in to examine the gravesite, he determines that Mori Okada's casket has not been opened, so his remains were not disturbed. But the sword that was displayed on top of the gravestone is gone.

MORI OKADA
BORN
DECEMBER 1, 1870
DIED
MAY 3, 1953

TRASH CAN FINDS

4 Near the gravesite is a trash can. On top of other trash, there's a pair of gloves and a fresh apple core.

SHOE & KNEE PRINTS

All around the grave, there are shoe and knee prints in the mud. Unfortunately, many of those probably belong to cemetery caretaker Henry Sato, who tromped all over the crime scene before police arrived.

5

6

SOIL & POLLEN

This crime scene is muddy and also covered in pollen from oak and sycamore trees that loom over the cemetery. Perhaps this trace evidence can help connect a suspect to the crime.

DO NOT CROSS

DO NOT CROSS

THE SUSPECTS

WHO WOULD WANT TO DISTURB A GREAT MAN'S FINAL RESTING PLACE? INVESTIGATORS INTERVIEWED BOTH YUNA OKADA AND CEMETERY CARETAKER HENRY SATO AND CAME UP WITH THE FOLLOWING LIST OF SUSPECTS:

HENRY SATO,
cemetery caretaker

MOTIVE: *Unknown*

But in failing to call the police immediately and instead investigating himself, Sato disturbed the crime scene and may have obscured evidence. It's possible that this was intentional, so that he could hide his involvement in the theft.

BERTHA O'BRIEN,
a local resident and antiques expert

MOTIVE: Interest in antiques

Investigators asked Yuna if she'd told anyone about the valuable sword displayed on her great-grandfather's gravestone. Yuna said she had recently been to an antiques value day at her public library, where experts gave the value of family artifacts. Yuna had showed O'Brien two of her great-grandfather's medals and mentioned the sword. O'Brien expressed great interest in this information.

MOTIVE: Historical significance

Yuna told investigators she'd recently attended a lecture by Vance, who asked if anyone in the audience had ancestors with connections to samurai culture. Yuna told Vance about her great-grandfather being buried with the old family treasure. Vance, too, asked many questions about the sword.

PETER VANCE,
a local historian

ANNA TANAKA,
Yuna Okada's niece

MOTIVE: Research

Yuna reported that her niece, Anna, was planning to visit Mori Okada's grave the night before. She was working on a project for her college history class and wanted to photograph the gravestone. If she did visit, she should have been the last person at the grave before Yuna discovered it had been disturbed.

DO NOT CRO

ROSS

BLOOD ANALYSIS

>>> **HENRY SATO'S EARLY INVESTIGATING OBSCURED MANY OF THE SHOE-PRINTS THAT YOU'D HOPED TO COLLECT FROM THE CRIME SCENE, BUT THERE ARE STILL SEVERAL SOLID PIECES OF EVIDENCE.**

The most promising of these is a smudge of what appears to be blood on the gravestone itself. Perhaps it can be tested for DNA. You'll need to obtain a sample to take back to the lab.

GATHER THE SAMPLE

To obtain the sample, investigators use a special cotton pad. It's been soaked in saline, a solution of water and salt. When blood cells are lifted from a surface with a saline solution, they are not damaged and can be analyzed. This pad has a convenient protective container that will prevent contamination until the sample gets to the lab.

IS IT BLOOD?

» Carefully, the technician takes the pad from the container and dabs it along the red smudge on the gravestone, collecting as much of the red substance as possible. He repeats the process with another pad.

» Back in the forensic blood analysis lab, the technician is waiting to help you check the sample to find out if it's actually blood. That's important because there's no sense in spending time and money to run a DNA test if the sample is just a smudge of ketchup or paint.

» The tech opens a vial of phenolphthalein and puts a few drops onto your sample. He adds a few drops of hydrogen peroxide to the pad, too.

✻ AND THE RESULTS SHOW … ✻

INSTANTLY, THE CHEMICAL MIX TURNS HOT PINK. A POSITIVE TEST RESULT! THAT MEANS THE SMUDGE ON THE GRAVESTONE IS BLOOD— QUITE POSSIBLY THE BLOOD OF THE PERSON WHO ROBBED MORI OKADA'S GRAVE.

? WHOSE BLOOD IS IT?

To find out more about whose blood it might be, you'll need to extract DNA from the sample. In the lab, this is a multistep process that involves using a centrifuge. That's the fast-spinning container that separates liquids of different densities. In this case, it will separate blood cells from plasma, or the liquid portion of blood. Once that's done, you go through several more steps to actually extract the DNA from the white blood cells. Once you've extracted the DNA from your blood sample, it's ready for the next step: amplification.

WHAT IS AMPLIFICATION?

In order to develop a DNA profile, a certain amount of DNA is required. This is accomplished by copying, or amplifying, the DNA that was isolated in the extraction step with a scientific technique referred to as the polymerase chain reaction, or PCR. During this process, specific strands of DNA are copied many times to create enough DNA for technicians to work with. Then, using a special process, the DNA strands are cut into segments of different lengths.

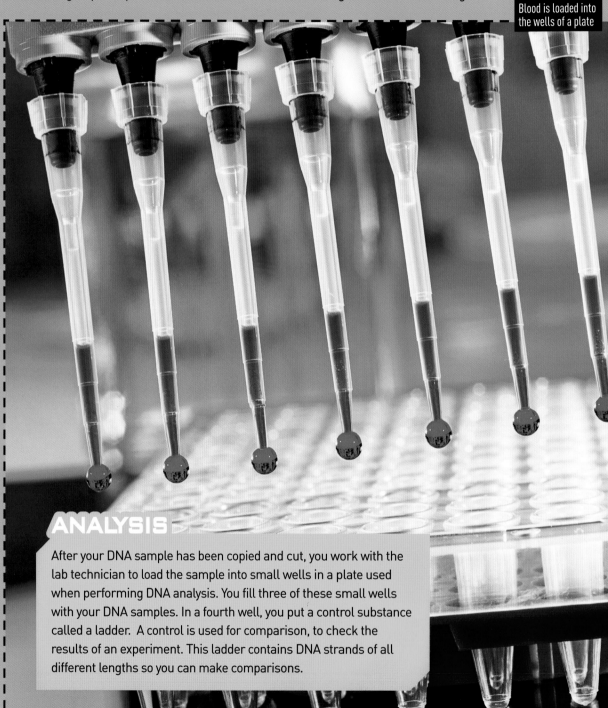

Blood is loaded into the wells of a plate

ANALYSIS

After your DNA sample has been copied and cut, you work with the lab technician to load the sample into small wells in a plate used when performing DNA analysis. You fill three of these small wells with your DNA samples. In a fourth well, you put a control substance called a ladder. A control is used for comparison, to check the results of an experiment. This ladder contains DNA strands of all different lengths so you can make comparisons.

DNA FINGERPRINT

Next, you load the plate onto an instrument called a genetic analyzer. The genetic analyzer sucks up your sample into a long thin tube called a capillary. The capillary is filled with very tiny beads and a liquid that can carry an electrical current. You attach wires from a power source to opposite sides of the capillary. Just like a battery, the wires have a positive and a negative side. You attach the negative side next to the beginning of the capillary and the positive side to the end. The electrical current pushes the DNA strands through the capillary. As the strands move through the capillary, they separate because the larger strands struggle to get through the tiny beads in the capillary and take longer to reach the end. The smaller strands can slip through the capillary more easily and will get to the end faster. This process is the same with your control strands from the ladder.

This whole setup is attached to a special computer that captures the pattern created when those DNA strands separate. That pattern is the DNA "fingerprint" of the person whose blood was on the gravestone. When it's ready, you and the lab technician enter your results into a database called the Combined DNA Index System, or CODIS.

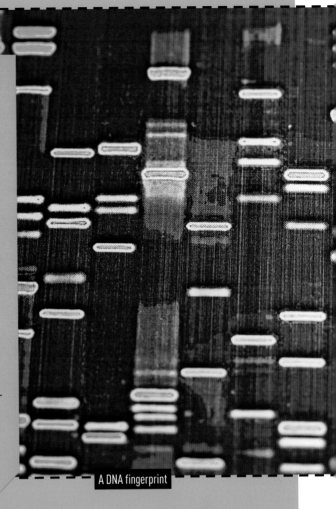

A DNA fingerprint

✱ AND THE RESULTS SHOW ... ✱

UNFORTUNATELY, YOUR SAMPLE DOESN'T MATCH ANY OF THE DNA SAMPLES CURRENTLY REGISTERED IN CODIS. THAT MEANS THAT WHOEVER'S BLOOD WAS ON THAT GRAVESTONE WASN'T IN THE SYSTEM.

CODIS only has certain kinds of DNA—from people who have been arrested or convicted of crimes, missing persons and their relatives, unidentified human remains, and unknown DNA found at crime scenes. So whose blood was on the gravestone? In order to find out if your sample matches the DNA of any of your suspects, you'll need them to submit blood samples. Perhaps they'll volunteer to do that, but it's more likely that you'll need to get a court order. And to do that, you'll need more evidence.

✱ For now, the DNA testing hasn't provided any answers. ✱

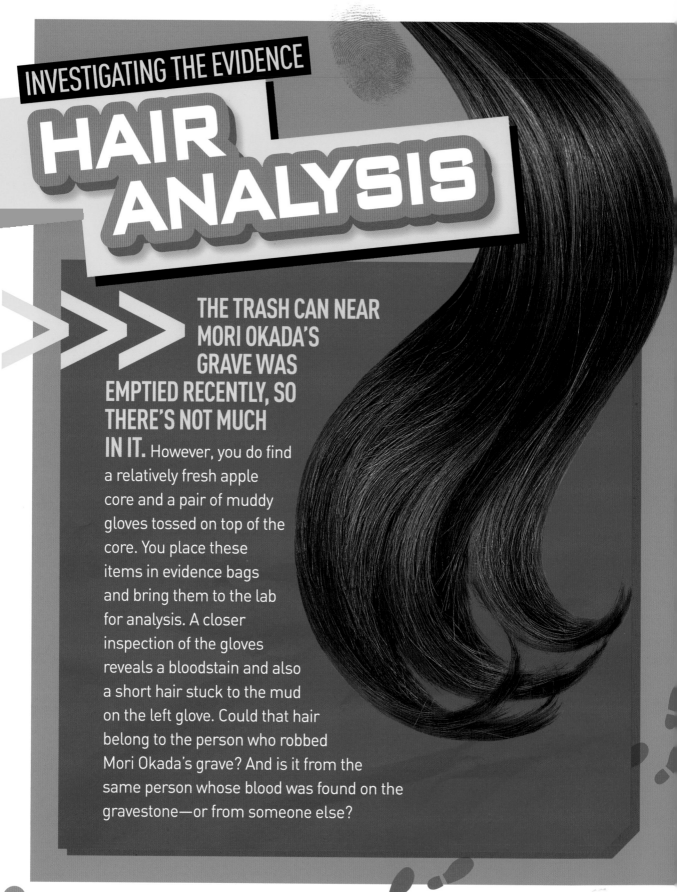

HAIR ANALYSIS

>>> **THE TRASH CAN NEAR MORI OKADA'S GRAVE WAS EMPTIED RECENTLY, SO THERE'S NOT MUCH IN IT.** However, you do find a relatively fresh apple core and a pair of muddy gloves tossed on top of the core. You place these items in evidence bags and bring them to the lab for analysis. A closer inspection of the gloves reveals a bloodstain and also a short hair stuck to the mud on the left glove. Could that hair belong to the person who robbed Mori Okada's grave? And is it from the same person whose blood was found on the gravestone—or from someone else?

GATHER YOUR SAMPLE

You take a sample of the blood and send it to the forensic blood analysis lab for DNA testing. You hope it will match the blood from the gravestone. But even if it does, that doesn't get you much closer to finding your suspect. You'd just know that they'd used gloves.

But every piece of evidence is important—even the smallest hair. Using forceps, so you don't accidentally transfer any of your own DNA to the sample, you carefully remove the hair from the muddy glove. You place it in a small container with a screw cap so the tiny hair doesn't get lost.

Sometimes hair that has been pulled out contains traces of DNA at its root. Like the blood sample, this might help provide a DNA match to the suspect. You take the hair to the lab so you can analyze it under the microscope and for DNA, if possible.

IS IT HUMAN?

Once again, you use forceps to remove the hair sample from the vial and transfer it to a microscope slide. You add a drop of water to keep it in place. Once you place a coverslip over the top of the hair and water, you're ready to take a closer look. You take a look at the medulla, the innermost area of the hair, which can be seen under the microscope. The medulla looks different in different species, and this one is definitely not a human medulla.

UNISERIAL (CATS)	
MULTISERIAL (RABBITS)	
VACUOLATED (DOGS, FOXES)	
LATTICE (DEER)	
AMORPHOUS (HUMAN)	

*AND THE RESULTS SHOW ... *

THIS HAIR ISN'T GOING TO BE AS HELPFUL AS YOU'D HOPED. IT'S OBVIOUSLY FROM AN ANIMAL—NOT A HUMAN. **THE MEDULLA IN HUMAN HAIR IS USUALLY THINNER, WHILE IN ANIMALS, IT CAN BE THIN OR THICK.**

Different kinds of medullas have different appearances, and it's pretty clear that the hair from the glove came from a dog. To confirm that conclusion, you notice that the root of this hair has a club shape, another feature that's found in dog hair but not human hair.

*Hopefully, your next piece of evidence will be more helpful in solving the crime. *

BITE MARK ANALYSIS

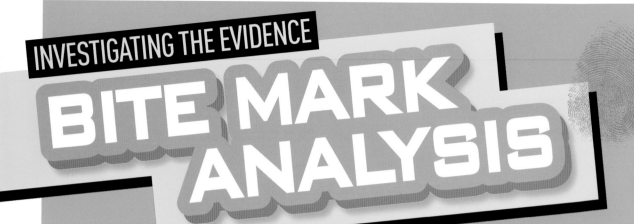

>>> **THE APPLE YOU FOUND IN THE TRASH CAN HAS OBVIOUS TEETH MARKS IN IT.**

If the bite mark analysis can link those marks to a person's dental records, that could help point to the culprit. You deliver the apple to the forensics lab. The bite marks in the apple still look fresh, and the apple has not yet begun to spoil, so you're off to a good start with this lead. You call in a forensic dentist, a professional who's an expert in identifying bite marks. Together, you photograph the bite marks in the apple. You include a ruler in the photographs so it's easy to see the size of the bite marks.

UNIQUE PATTERNS

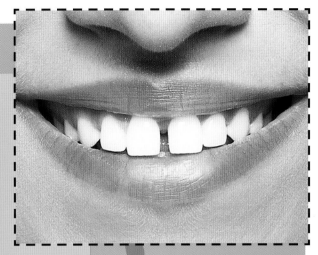

This could be a great lead—you have already noticed that the tooth pattern on this apple is fairly unique. The marks indicate that there's a gap between the person's two top middle teeth and that their bottom teeth are quite crooked.

When forensic dentists study bite marks, they're looking for other details, too. If a biter's tooth is chipped, then it will make a jagged impression, and a person with braces will leave a different sort of mark, too.

If you have enough evidence pointing to one of your suspects, you might be able to get a judge to issue an order to take a mold of their teeth. Then you can compare that mold with photographs of the bite marks in the apple to look for similarities.

* AND THE RESULTS SHOW ... *

WHEN YOU DESCRIBE THE BITE MARK PHOTOGRAPHS TO YUNA OKADA, SHE HAS AN IDEA RIGHT AWAY. "THAT'S A PERFECT DESCRIPTION OF MY NIECE'S TEETH," SHE SAYS. "I'VE ALWAYS LOVED HER UNIQUE SMILE."

ANNA TANAKA,
Yuna Okada's niece

Sure enough, when you interview Anna Tanaka about her visit to the cemetery, she says she was indeed eating an apple when she arrived to visit Mori Okada's gravesite. With that information, there's no need to make a mold of anyone's teeth. The mystery of the discarded apple, at least, is solved.

But Anna says the grave was in fine shape when she saw it, and she didn't see anyone else in the cemetery when she left. She says she tossed her apple in the trash can as she was leaving. You ask Anna if she also discarded the gloves there, and she says she didn't. She didn't look in the trash can when she threw the apple away, so she can't say if the gloves were present at that time or not.

However, the gloves were draped over the apple, so if they belonged to the robber, it's likely that whoever robbed Mori Okada's grave was there after Anna left for the evening.

* Let's see what other evidence we found. *

99

INVESTIGATING THE EVIDENCE

SOIL & POLLEN ANALYSIS

>>> **SO FAR, YOU BELIEVE ANNA'S STORY, SINCE IT MATCHES UP WITH THE EVIDENCE YOU HAVE.**

But you need something more concrete to rule her out as a suspect entirely and to find the real culprit. Bertha O'Brien's neighbors say she loves to garden, so it's no surprise to see her with muddy pants when you go to interview her. Peter Vance was seen at a restaurant late last night in dirty jeans. He told a friend it was from the floor of his garage and his wife's flower garden, as he'd been working on his car and doing yard work all day. And Henry Sato, who digs graves and maintains the gardens in the cemetery, is always muddy after a workday.

SOIL COMPONENTS

But there's a way to determine which mud came from the gravesite and which mud came from somewhere else. You take a sample of mud from the grave and bring it to the lab for soil analysis. Once you arrive, you examine the soil under a microscope to check for distinguishing characteristics that might have a unique color and consistency, like shell fragments, pollen granules, or the presence of clay.

Clay

Pollen

Shell fragments

Shell fragments would suggest the soil was in an area that may have been a pond or lake at one time. The area in which the cemetery is located used to be wetlands a long time ago, so you're not surprised when you see small, brownish fragments and, periodically, a white piece of shell, too. There are also pollen granules, which is what interests you the most.

Earlier in the day, you paid a visit to O'Brien's garden, which is right along a public sidewalk. As you collected a quick soil sample, you noticed that her street is lined with sugar maple trees. The cemetery is in a different part of town, where oak and sycamore trees tower over the graves. Not surprisingly, the pollen samples taken from the gravesite are consistent with pollen from oak and sycamore trees.

GATHER SAMPLES

Now you just need samples from the clothing of your suspects. Henry Sato offers to let you scrape some mud off his work pants, but there's no point in that since his daily work involves digging in the cemetery. Of course the soil and pollen will match. You're more interested in the dirt from Peter Vance's muddy pants and the dirt under Bertha O'Brien's fingernails. You pay a visit to O'Brien. She says she's embarrassed by her fingernails—they're always dirty!—but she's happy to cooperate and provide a sample for you to take back to the lab.

MORE CLUES

Vance isn't home when you knock on his door, so you drop by the restaurant where he was seen last night. He's not there either, but the owner has just arrived to clean up from the night before. She lets you inside and shows you where Vance was sitting, and you notice that there's quite a bit of dried mud on the floor beneath his chair. You collect some of it and put it into a vial. There's also a bandage on the floor with a bit of dried blood on it. The restaurant owner recalls that Vance had a cut on his hand and had asked her for a new bandage after the old one fell off. You collect that, too, and place it in an evidence bag.

Back at the forensics lab, under the microscope you discover that the soil sample from underneath Bertha O'Brien's fingernails looks nothing like your sample from the cemetery. The pollen is different and the soil is much finer.

BERTHA O'BRIEN,
a local resident and antiques expert

Graveyard sample with sycamore pollen

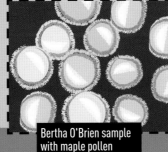

Bertha O'Brien sample with maple pollen

✻ AND THE RESULTS SHOW … ✻

WHEN YOU PUT THIS SAMPLE UNDER THE MICROSCOPE, **THE SOIL AND POLLEN GRANULES TELL A DIFFERENT STORY.**

Peter Vance sample

Peter Vance lives in the same part of town as O'Brien. If he was telling the truth about working on his car in the garage and doing yard work, the soil from his pants should look a lot like O'Brien's sample, mixed with some oil residue from the garage floor.

✻ Let's gather everything we know so far. ✻

HERE'S ANOTHER LOOK AT YOUR SUSPECTS, ALONG WITH THE EVIDENCE AND OTHER INFORMATION GATHERED SO FAR. **TAKE A FEW MINUTES TO REVIEW, AND THEN SEE IF YOU CAN DETERMINE WHO THE CULPRIT IS!**

MORI
OKADA
BORN
DECEMBER 1, 1870
DIED
MAY 3, 1953

HENRY SATO,
cemetery caretaker

MOTIVE: Unknown

It's unclear what Sato's motive might have been, or how he would have known how valuable the sword is. But as cemetery caretaker, he certainly had access to the grave, and his hands and knees were muddy. He didn't call the police right away when the crime was reported. Could this have been an attempt to hide his guilt?

BERTHA O'BRIEN,
a local resident and antiques expert

MOTIVE: Interest in antiques

Bertha O'Brien knew that Mori Okada was buried with the sword, and she understood how valuable it was. She'd been seen with muddy hands and knees, but soil samples showed that the mud likely came from her own garden and didn't match the samples taken from the cemetery.

MOTIVE: Historical significance

Like Bertha O'Brien, Peter Vance knew about the sword buried with Mori Okada and had been seen with muddy knees on the day the crime was committed. He'd told investigators it was from his garage and his wife's garden, but the mud found near his seat at the restaurant was a clear match with the sample taken from the cemetery. Vance also had an injury on his hand that night, and the bandage found near his seat at the restaurant is currently being tested for DNA to see if it matches the blood found on the gravestone.

PETER VANCE,
a local historian

ANNA TANAKA,
Yuna Okada's niece

MOTIVE: Research

Anna Tanaka was the last person to visit Mori Okada's grave before the sword was discovered missing. Her teeth matched the bite marks in the half-eaten apple found near the site, and she admitted she'd been there and had thrown away the apple.

✻ Who do you think DID IT?
Turn the page to find out! ✻

AND THE CULPRIT IS ...

🙁 PETER VANCE

After your soil samples revealed that Vance wasn't telling the truth about his muddy pants, you return to the forensic blood analysis lab—this time with the bloody bandage from Vance's seat at the restaurant.

SOLVED

IT'S NOT EASY WAITING FOR DNA RESULTS TO COME BACK WHEN YOU'RE SO CLOSE TO SOLVING A CRIME, BUT IT'S IMPORTANT TO HAVE A STRONG CASE. Sure enough, when the DNA sample comes up on the computer, it's a match for the sample collected from the blood on the gravestone and also matches the blood found on the gloves from the trash can. Armed with that evidence, you return to Peter Vance's house to place him under arrest. His dog, a large German shepherd, barks like mad when you ring the doorbell. Vance doesn't look surprised to see you. Confronted with the evidence, he confesses that after hearing Yuna's story about her great-grandfather's priceless samurai sword, he went to the cemetery late at night to steal it. He brought his dog so he'd know if anyone was coming, which explains the dog hair on the glove. Vance admits that he'd planned to sell the sword in an online auction but hadn't even had a chance to photograph it yet. He leads you to his kitchen, where Mori Okada's sword sits on the dining table, still speckled with mud.

A CLOSER LOOK

DNA ANALYSIS

>> **DNA ANALYSIS HAS ONLY BEEN USED IN CRIMINAL INVESTIGATIONS SINCE THE LATE 1980S, BUT THE RESEARCH THAT LED TO THIS BREAKTHROUGH GOES BACK MUCH FARTHER.** It includes work done in the 1800s by scientists like Charles Darwin, who noticed that living things pass on traits to their offspring; Gregor Mendel, who learned more about how genes work; and Johann Friedrich Miescher, who first identified DNA in human cells. (He called it "nuclein" back then.)

THE FIRST PHOTO

In the 1900s, there were more developments. Austrian scientist Karl Landsteiner won the Nobel Prize in 1900 for developing the ABO blood typing system. The test that uses phenolphthalein to detect blood was developed around the same time. And in 1952, British scientist Rosalind Franklin first photographed DNA. Her research paved the way for the discovery of DNA's double helix structure, which James Watson and Francis Crick wrote about in 1953.

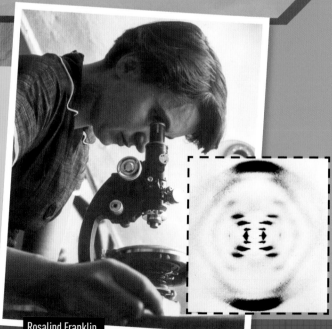

Rosalind Franklin

ALEC JEFFREYS

In 1984, British researcher Alec Jeffreys was working on a project about inherited illnesses when he accidentally produced the world's first DNA fingerprint—those unique patterns in DNA. When he developed some film of repeated sections of DNA, Jeffreys realized that every individual in his study had a different pattern. Within a couple of years, DNA fingerprinting technology was put to use in crime labs in Britain and the United States.

Real-World CRIME SCIENCE!

Today, DNA test results are often used in courtrooms, where suspects are on trial for various crimes. But the evidence doesn't always prove a person is guilty. Sometimes, DNA can prove innocence when someone has been wrongly accused of a crime.

This happened for the first time way back in 1987, not long after Alec Jeffreys published his research about DNA fingerprints. Police in Leicestershire, England, had arrested a suspect in a case and wanted Jeffreys to help them connect him to the crimes. So Jeffreys ran some DNA samples—one from the suspect and two taken from the victims. He discovered that the same person was responsible for the crimes, but that person was not the suspect the police had arrested. Based on that evidence, the police released that suspect and later arrested the real culprit.

DNA EVIDENCE CAN ALSO BE USED TO OVERTURN CONVICTIONS IN COURT CASES THAT HAPPENED BEFORE THE TECHNOLOGY WAS AVAILABLE. **SINCE 1989, MORE THAN 150 PEOPLE IMPRISONED IN THE UNITED STATES HAVE BEEN PROVEN INNOCENT, THANKS TO DNA TESTING.**

EXTRACTING DNA FROM A STRAWBERRY

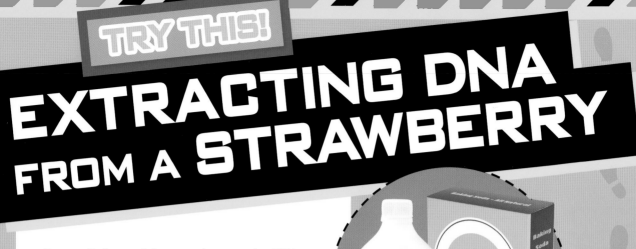

Every cell of every living organism contains DNA, the code of life for that species. But in order to analyze DNA, scientists need to free its long, coiled strands from the cell. The following procedure contains the same basic steps a forensic scientist would use to extract DNA from white blood cells or skin cells.

✷ Are you ready to extract DNA from a strawberry? ✷

ADULT SUPERVISION REQUIRED:

Use of heat source

>> WHAT YOU'LL NEED

- A fresh strawberry
- A small bowl
- A fork or potato masher
- ¼ cup (60 mL) of water
- A hot plate or stove (an electric burner is best)
- A heat resistant glass container that can be used on a stove top
- Pot holders to hold the glass container
- A Fahrenheit or Celsius candy thermometer
- 2 tablespoons (30 mL) of dish soap
- Baking soda
- 1 tablespoon (13 g) of meat tenderizer powder (can be found in the spice aisle at a grocery store)
- A test tube or other narrow, clear glass container (like a tall, narrow glass)
- Rubbing alcohol
- A timer or clock
- A toothpick

>> PROCEDURE

1 Ask an adult to cut the stem off the strawberry. Then crush the strawberry gently in the small bowl with the fork or potato masher. It can still be a little lumpy.

2 Add the water to the strawberry sample. Put the mixture in the heat resistant glassware and have an adult use the hot plate or stove burner to bring this sample to a temperature of 120 to 140°F (50–60°C). **Be sure your sample remains in that temperature range throughout the process.** Do not allow the sample temperature to go above 140°F (60°C). That would damage the DNA.

1

2

Continued

3 Add the dish soap and stir constantly for five minutes. Be sure the temperature remains between 120 to 140°F (50–60°C). You may need to remove the glassware from the heat source periodically to maintain the temperature. (Be sure to use pot holders!)

4 Add two pinches of baking soda and stir briefly.

5 Add the meat tenderizer powder and stir constantly for two minutes.

6 Have the adult place the container on a heat resistant surface. Allow the solids to settle to the bottom of the container.

7 Have the adult pour some of the liquid portion into the test tube (or other narrow glass container) until the test tube is about 2/3 full.

8 Gently, and **very slowly,** add the rubbing alcohol, allowing it to flow down the side of the test tube so it layers on top of your mixture. Add enough so that you can see a layer of clear alcohol, about an inch (2–3 cm) thick. Then, allow it to sit without disturbing it. Within five to seven minutes, you should see pure DNA rise through the rubbing alcohol and up to the surface of the mixture like a ghostly collection of strands. Dip your toothpick into the test tube and you may find that some of those strands stick to it. Congratulations! You've isolated some strawberry DNA.

THIS SAME ACTIVITY WORKS WHEN REMOVING DNA FROM RAW WHEAT GERM!

3

4

7

8

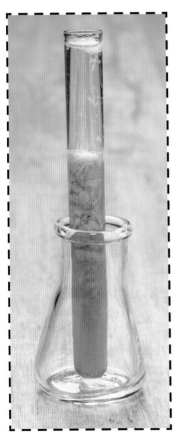

>> HOW IT WORKS

Cell membranes and nuclear membranes are made of double layers of lipids, or fats. The dish soap breaks down the fatty layers and frees the DNA, which is found in chromosomes in the nucleus of the cell. Once the DNA has been freed, the meat tenderizer further straightens the DNA strands by breaking apart the tangled knots. Finally, the DNA, which doesn't dissolve easily in rubbing alcohol, is free to rise up to the top of the mixture.

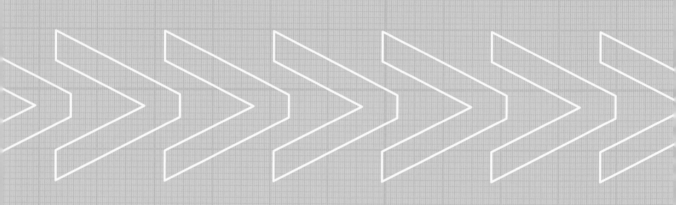

STOLEN BONES

MISSING

THE SCENARIO

SITUATION NOTES:

Dr. Hena Patel, a forensic anthropologist at the Museum of Natural History,
arrived at work after a month-long
research trip to Australia to find her
office had been burglarized. Someone
had smashed its second-story window,
but no one is sure when it happened.
No one noticed the break-in until
Patel returned home. Her computer
and other expensive electronics were
just as she'd left them. But someone
did steal a box of bones—human remains
that were already at the center of
a controversy.

THE STORY OF THE BONES

CONSTRUCTION SITE

Ronald Park's real estate company, Purple Meadow Properties, has been planning a new apartment complex for more than five years. Finally, this past spring, the final paperwork was approved. An old farmhouse on the planned building site was knocked down, and Park's crew cleared the debris and broke ground on the project. Within a week, though, digging had to stop because one of the backhoes had unearthed human bones. The project foreman immediately called the police. What if there had been a murder? As soon as investigators arrived, they realized they weren't dealing with a murder—or at least not a recent one. The location of the bones, underneath an addition that had been built onto the original home in 1920, suggested that the bones were older than any of the people who had uncovered them.

BONES

Whose bones are they? Are there more nearby? Can the construction project continue? And what should happen to those bones?

THE LAND

The owner of the original house, who'd sold both the building and the land to Purple Meadow Properties, believes that the bones may belong to one of her relatives who built the original farmhouse back in the 1800s. She'd heard family stories about her great-great-uncle Theodore being buried on the property but never thought his remains would be found. She requested the bones so that she could have them buried in the family cemetery plot where her other relatives are laid to rest.

But that land is also the ancestral homeland of a local Native American Tribe. A federal law called the Native American Graves Protection and Repatriation Act requires that all Tribal nations be notified when any remains are found in their ancestral homelands. As soon as the bones were found, the Tribal Historic Preservation Officer, who's responsible for the enforcement of preservation laws, requested that the bones be turned over to the Tribe. Tribal leaders say the farmhouse was built on land that may have served as a burial ground for their ancestors. They requested that the bones be returned immediately for a proper burial according to their Tribal customs.

But before the bones could be turned over to either the family or the Tribe, a judge ordered a complete analysis of the bones to be conducted by experts at the Museum of Natural History.

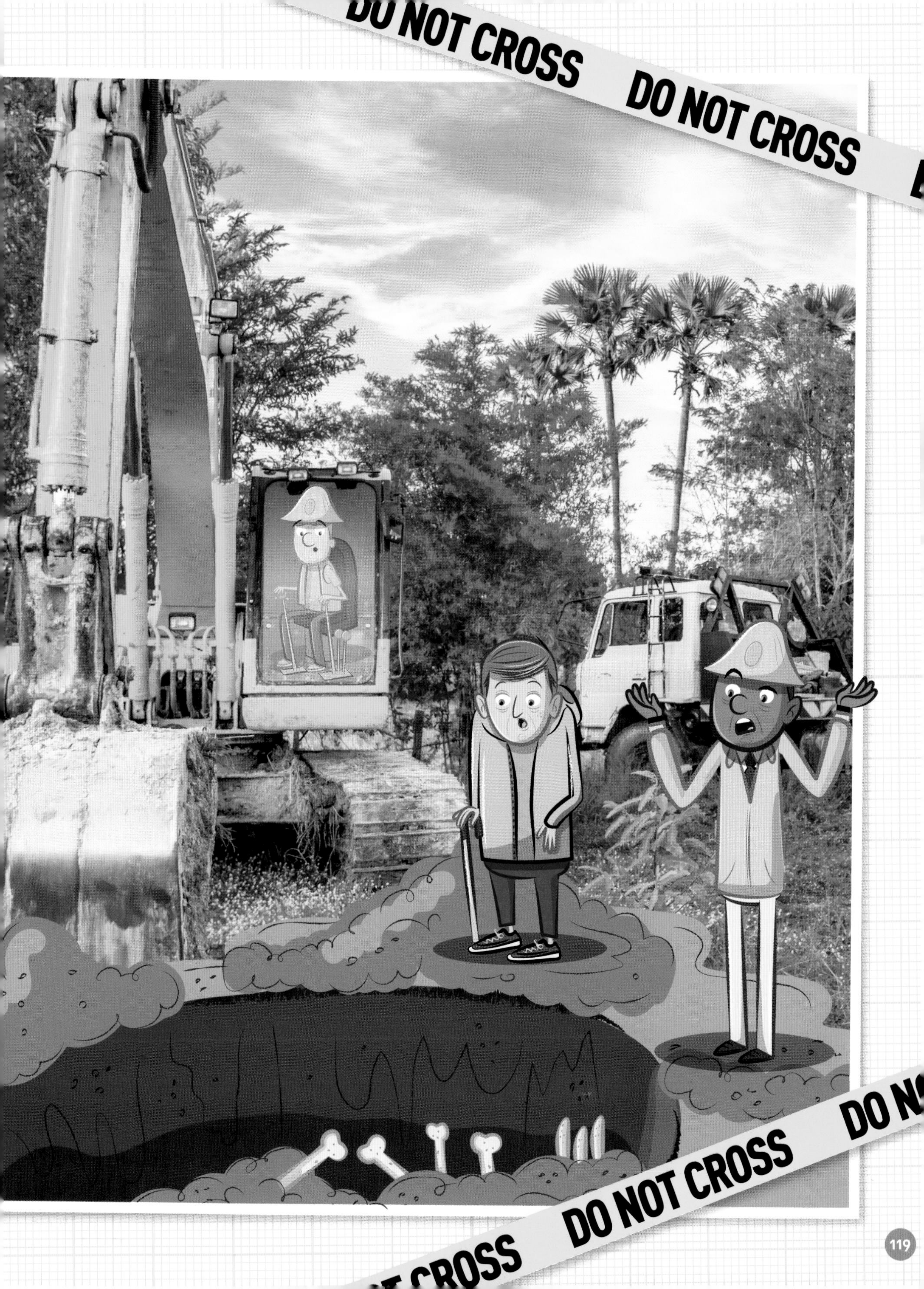
DO NOT CROSS
DO NOT CROSS
DO NOT CROSS
DO NOT CROSS

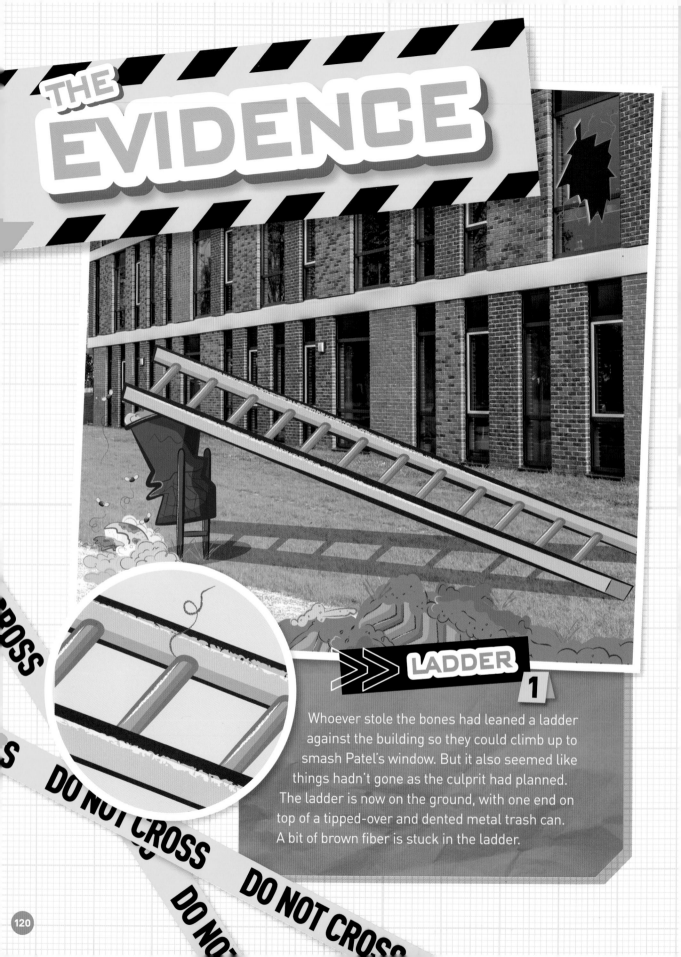

THE EVIDENCE

>> LADDER 1

Whoever stole the bones had leaned a ladder against the building so they could climb up to smash Patel's window. But it also seemed like things hadn't gone as the culprit had planned. The ladder is now on the ground, with one end on top of a tipped-over and dented metal trash can. A bit of brown fiber is stuck in the ladder.

DO NOT CROSS

TRASH 2

The trash can's contents have spilled onto the dirt. They are mostly old papers and food wrappers, but there is also half of a roast beef sandwich that seems like it might have been thrown away more recently.

3 TIRE TRACKS

Tire tracks in the dried mud indicate the culprit likely drove away.

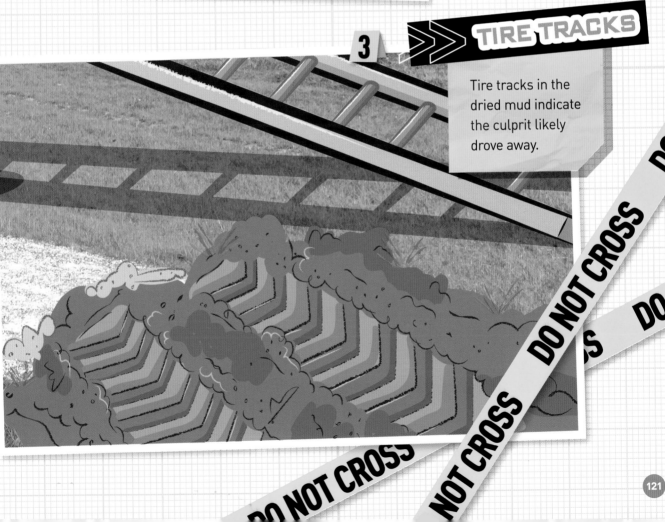

DO NOT CROSS

THE SUSPECTS

WHO WOULD STEAL A BOX OF BONES? INVESTIGATORS INTERVIEWED ADMINISTRATORS AT THE MUSEUM AND REVIEWED NEWSPAPER STORIES ABOUT THE DISCOVERY OF THESE BONES TO COME UP WITH A LIST OF SUSPECTS.

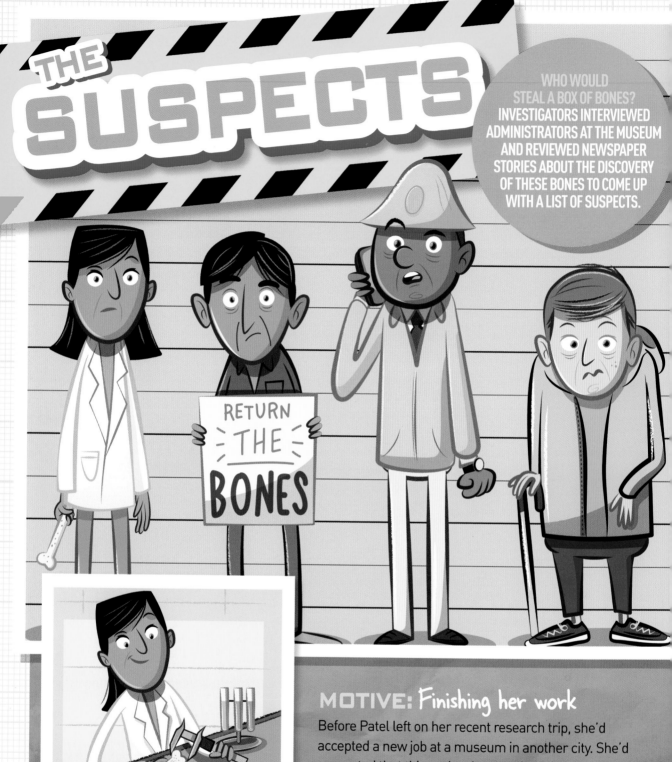

RETURN THE BONES

DR. HENA PATEL,
forensic anthropologist at the
Museum of Natural History

MOTIVE: Finishing her work

Before Patel left on her recent research trip, she'd accepted a new job at a museum in another city. She'd requested that this project be transferred along with her, but that request was denied. Patel argued that this was her investigation—one she did not want to leave to another scientist. But the museum's decision was final. Could Patel have staged the burglary to cover up the fact that she stole the bones herself, before she left for her new job?

MOTIVE: Money

The discovery of the contested bones led a judge to order that Park and his team stop all work on their construction project until more information could be learned. Park was furious and claimed he was losing money every day the project was delayed. Investigators wonder if he stole the bones to put an end to the whole matter. He says he has an alibi, however, as he claims to have been out of town for a week when the burglary was discovered.

RONALD PARK,
president of Purple Meadow Properties

MOTIVE: Activism

Max Williams is a Native leader and activist who is frustrated with the government's response to the discovery of these bones. The Tribe opposes scientific testing of the bones, and Williams has made it clear that he does not appreciate the museum's delays in determining their origins. Police believe Williams may have stolen the bones in an act of civil disobedience.

MAX WILLIAMS,
a Native activist

HELEN MCCAIN,
former owner of the farmhouse on the current Purple Meadow property

MOTIVE: Family history

McCain has told investigators that she is certain the bones discovered during the construction project belong to one of her ancestors, and she's requested that they be returned for burial in a family cemetery plot. Like Williams, she has grown increasingly impatient with the museum. She's an older woman who doesn't get around very well anymore, but might she have had a partner in the heist, or hired someone to steal the bones for her?

TIRE PRINT ANALYSIS

INVESTIGATORS BELIEVE THAT THE TIRE PRINTS LEFT IN THE DRIED MUD BELOW HENA PATEL'S WINDOW may be their best hope of catching the person who broke into her office. That's the first piece of evidence you'll investigate.

OBSERVE AND RECORD

First, you walk all around the tire tracks in the dried mud, snapping photographs as you go. It's important to take pictures from directly above the print, and close-ups, too. You put a white ruler down across the tracks for scale so that investigators can see exactly how big across the tire marks are. Sometimes the make and model of a car can be figured out by the tires. Sometimes individual tires even have a small gouge or stone in them. Those might appear in the cast of the tire print, making it even easier to pinpoint which tire left the print.

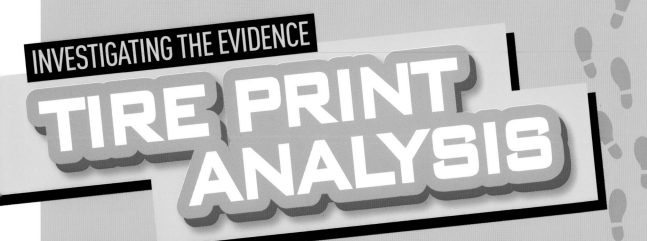

MAKE A MODEL

After you take photographs of the tire prints and the surrounding area, you remove an impression mold kit from your bag and mix the plaster with water to create a gooey paste.

» Slowly and carefully, you pour that mixture into both tire tracks. After the plaster hardens, you remove it and attach the casts of the tread tracks onto large pieces of cardboard.

» Then you take them to the lab for a computer match to a tire brand, and maybe even to a car make and model.

In the lab, you work with a technician to see if there's a match. First, you call up a special database of tire treads. You upload your images into the computer and program some identifying features. This will tell the program what to look for. You wait while the computer processes the information.

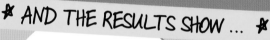

✱ AND THE RESULTS SHOW ... ✱

THERE'S BOTH GOOD NEWS AND BAD NEWS. **THE COMPUTER HAS MADE A MATCH! UNFORTUNATELY, THIS TIRE IS A VERY COMMON ONE.** BUT AT LEAST IT'S A START.

This kind of tire is common on medium- and heavy-duty pickup trucks made to handle towing and to carry heavy cargo. Do any of your suspects have a truck like that?

If you're able to find the vehicle that you think made these tire tracks, you'll need to compare that vehicle's tire tracks to those at the crime scene. To do that, you'll put ink on the suspect vehicle's tires and drive them over paper. Then you'll be able to perform side-by-side comparisons by placing that vehicle's tracks alongside the crime scene tracks. You'll examine the same areas on both and look for matching characteristics, including any unique marks.

YOU DO A BIT MORE INVESTIGATING AND FIND OUT THAT BOTH HENA PATEL AND RONALD PARK DRIVE VEHICLES LIKE THAT, **AND THEIR TRUCKS HAVE ALMOST IDENTICAL TIRES. IT'S A SOLID LEAD, BUT IT'S NOT ENOUGH.**

✱ You decide to take a closer look at the sandwich from the trash. ✱

FORENSIC ENTOMOLOGY

SOMETIMES, KNOWING WHEN A CRIME HAPPENED IS IMPORTANT WHEN IT COMES TO FIGURING OUT WHO COMMITTED THAT CRIME. In this case, both Hena Patel and Ronald Park were out of town for a period of time before the break-in at the museum office was discovered. Fortunately, there's evidence that can help determine when the break-in happened—half of a roast beef sandwich. The sandwich seems more recent than other garbage from the trash can, but it's obviously been there a while. The meat inside stinks and is swarming with flies.

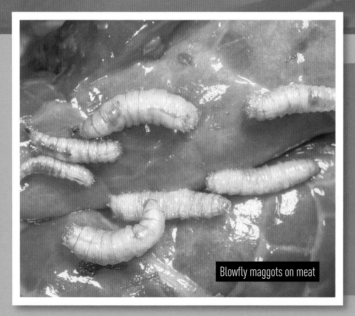

Blowfly maggots on meat

Believe it or not, those flies are also a clue. Blowflies, the most common insects found on rotting meat, have an amazing sense of smell. They can detect blood and decomposition from more than 300 feet (91 m) away, and because of this, they tend to colonize any sort of dead tissue very quickly, whether it's a dead body or meat in an old sandwich.

WHAT IS ENTOMOLOGY?

Entomology is the study of insects. When that science is applied to the investigation of a crime, we call it forensic entomology.

BLOWFLIES

Female blowflies lay eggs almost as soon as they arrive on decaying meat. In a day, those eggs hatch into maggots and begin to eat the meat. Over the next four days or so, the maggots grow from their original size of about 0.08 inches (2 mm) to about 0.8 inches (20 mm). Once a maggot is fully grown, it finds a dark place and becomes a pupa. Ten days later, it will hatch as an adult fly. When a female fly is two days old, she will lay eggs, and the process starts all over again.

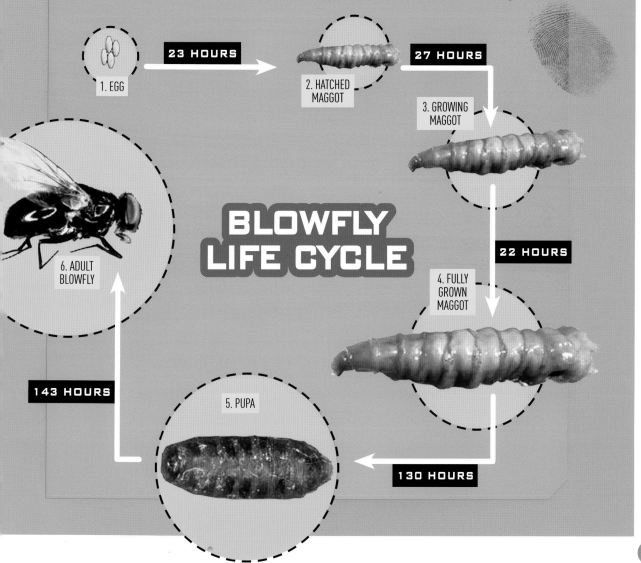

BLOWFLY LIFE CYCLE

1. EGG

23 HOURS

2. HATCHED MAGGOT

27 HOURS

3. GROWING MAGGOT

22 HOURS

4. FULLY GROWN MAGGOT

130 HOURS

5. PUPA

143 HOURS

6. ADULT BLOWFLY

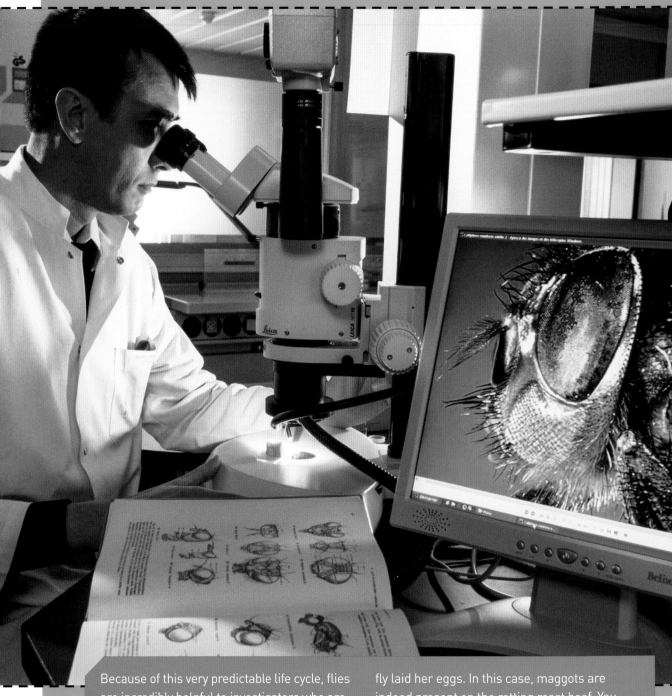

Because of this very predictable life cycle, flies are incredibly helpful to investigators who are trying to find out when a crime took place. They look for maggots as well as pupae in the soil or other dark areas nearby. Studying these allows experts to backtrack to the time when the first fly laid her eggs. In this case, maggots are indeed present on the rotting roast beef. You hope they'll be able to help pinpoint when the sandwich was discarded, which might help to rule out a suspect. It's time to call in a forensic entomologist.

You work with the forensic entomologist to collect a large amount of larvae and maggots from the rotting meat in the sandwich. If you have a good sample of each species and the stages of their development, you'll have a better idea how long ago the sandwich was discarded. Carefully, you pluck some of the white, wormlike maggots from the roast beef and place them in a container with some preservative. You also remove a brown pupa from the bottom of the overturned garbage can. Looking at what you've collected so far, the forensic entomologist is already able to offer some thoughts.

* AND THE RESULTS SHOW ... *

BECAUSE YOU'VE FOUND MANY PUPA CASINGS AND FEWER TINY MAGGOT BABIES, IT LOOKS LIKE THAT SANDWICH HAS BEEN IN THE GARBAGE FOR ABOUT 7 TO 10 DAYS AT THE MOST.

If the sandwich was thrown away much more recently, you wouldn't be seeing the pupae, just eggs and maggots. If it had been there much longer, you'd probably be seeing some different kinds of insects along with the flies, like certain kinds of beetles and mites that tend to arrive later in the decomposition process. All of this is based on the recent weather, too. If the air temperature recently had been cooler, you'd revise your estimate to around 20 days, since a fly's life cycle is longer in colder temperatures. But recently, the temperatures have been quite warm and muggy. So 7 to 10 days ago is your best guess for when the sandwich was discarded, which probably means that's when the crime was committed, too.

That means there's no way Hena Patel could have staged this crime before leaving on her trip to Australia a month ago.

DR. HENA PATEL,
forensic anthropologist at the Museum of Natural History

IT ALSO MEANS THAT RONALD PARK'S ALIBI—BEING AWAY FOR THE PAST WEEK—ISN'T SUCH A PERFECT ALIBI AFTER ALL.

NEW!

RONALD PARK,
president of Purple Meadow Properties

* But you'll need more evidence to know for sure if he's the burglar. *

FIBER ANALYSIS

THE LADDER FOUND AT THE CRIME SCENE DIDN'T BELONG TO THE MUSEUM OF NATURAL HISTORY. That means whoever broke into Dr. Hena Patel's office must have brought it with them, most likely in the same truck that left those tire tracks.

Investigators at the crime scene noticed some brown fiber from clothing or carpet was stuck on one of the ladder's screws, and they're hoping that last clue might pin down the culprit. Fibers found at a crime scene can sometimes be matched with a person's clothing, connecting them to the crime. Your investigation reveals that Ronald Park frequently wears a brown construction-type jacket and was recently seen with a rip in his sleeve. Could it be that he caught it in the ladder on the night of the crime?

RONALD PARK,
president of Purple Meadow Properties

GATHER SAMPLES

Based on that report and the other evidence you have so far, a judge issues a search warrant for Park's home. You find the brown jacket in his closet and take it to the forensic science lab for analysis, along with that fiber sample found on the ladder.

UNDER A MICROSCOPE

At the lab, you place a fiber sample from Park's jacket and the fabric from the ladder side by side under a microscope. The color matches exactly. And when you study the weave pattern, you see similarities, too. The two fibers show the same curly over-under weave pattern in the same shade of brown.

THERMAL DECOMPOSITION

There's another test you'd like to have done on these samples, and it relates to thermal decomposition—the temperature at which different substances break down. It could be helpful in confirming that these two fibers match. That's because the chemistry of different kinds of fibers can cause them to burn in different ways.

You take your two fiber samples from under the microscope and cut a small piece from each. Next, a technician picks up each piece with a pair of forceps— one in his right hand and one in his left. He lights a Bunsen burner and puts both samples into the flame at the same time. You'll see a distinct burn color for each one, and that will allow you to compare the flames. In this case, they're identical. You blow out the flame on each fiber and then check to see if they smell the same. One at a time, you wave each piece carefully in the air near your nose and take a whiff of the smell produced by the singed fibers. Both smell like paper, and this is typical for cotton. The residue left behind is a white, fluffy ash rather than the melted black bead that's left behind when synthetic fibers burn. That means neither of the fibers is human-made, another sign that you're dealing with cotton. This "sniff test" probably can't be used in court, but it helps to confirm what you learned from the other fiber analysis.

BASED ON THIS AND THE MICROSCOPE IMAGES, YOU CONCLUDE THAT BOTH FIBERS ARE THE KIND OF COTTON CANVAS FROM PARK'S JACKET.

✷ Let's gather everything we know so far. ✷

HERE'S ANOTHER LOOK AT YOUR SUSPECTS, ALONG WITH THE EVIDENCE AND OTHER INFORMATION GATHERED SO FAR. TAKE A FEW MINUTES TO REVIEW, AND THEN SEE IF YOU CAN DETERMINE WHO THE CULPRIT IS!

MOTIVE: Finishing her work

Patel's desire to keep working with the bones in her new job is a possible motive, and she does have the kind of truck that may have left those tire prints. However, Patel was out of town for a month, and the forensic entomology results show that the sandwich left at the crime scene had been there only 7 to 10 days.

DR. HENA PATEL,
forensic anthropologist at the Museum of Natural History

RONALD PARK,
president of Purple Meadow Properties

MOTIVE: Money

Park's motive is clear—he wanted to continue building his new apartment complex. He drives the same sort of truck that left the tire prints, and his jacket matched the fiber samples taken from the ladder at the crime scene. Park's alibi, being out of town for a week, doesn't rule him out as a suspect because your forensic entomology results suggest that the crime scene roast beef sandwich may have been dropped there before Park left for his trip.

MOTIVE: Activism

Williams has been frustrated that the bones haven't been turned over to the Tribe, and this could give him a motive to have stolen them. But Williams drives a small, two-door car that wouldn't fit a ladder and doesn't match the tire tracks found at the crime scene. Could he have borrowed a truck on the day the crime was committed?

MAX WILLIAMS,
a Native activist

HELEN MCCAIN,
former owner of the farmhouse on the current Purple Meadow property

MOTIVE: Family history

McCain's motive is a desire to take possession of the bones that she believes belong to her ancestor. McCain doesn't have a car, as she gave up driving last year, but her son often takes her places. He drives a station wagon—not the kind of vehicle that left the tire prints.

✲ Who do you think DID IT? Turn the page to find out! ✲

THE SOLUTION

AND THE CULPRIT IS ...

☹ RONALD PARK!

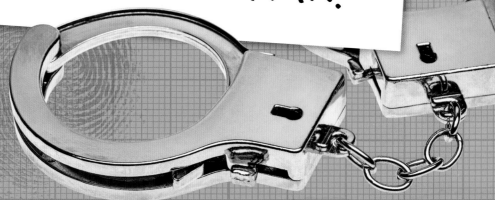

Your forensic entomology work in this case ruled out Patel as a suspect because she was clearly out of the country at the time this crime occurred. Park, however, was still very much a suspect based on that insect evidence.

SOLVED

THE TIRE TRACKS AT THE CRIME SCENE MATCHED THE TIRES ON HIS TRUCK, AND THE FIBER CAUGHT IN THE LADDER WAS A PERFECT MATCH WITH THE BROWN COTTON CANVAS FROM HIS TORN JACKET.

Confronted with this evidence, Park confessed to the break-in. He admitted that he stole the bones in order to put an end to his construction troubles because he was losing so much money with every week the project was delayed. Park returned the box of bones immediately, leaving one more big forensic question to be answered.

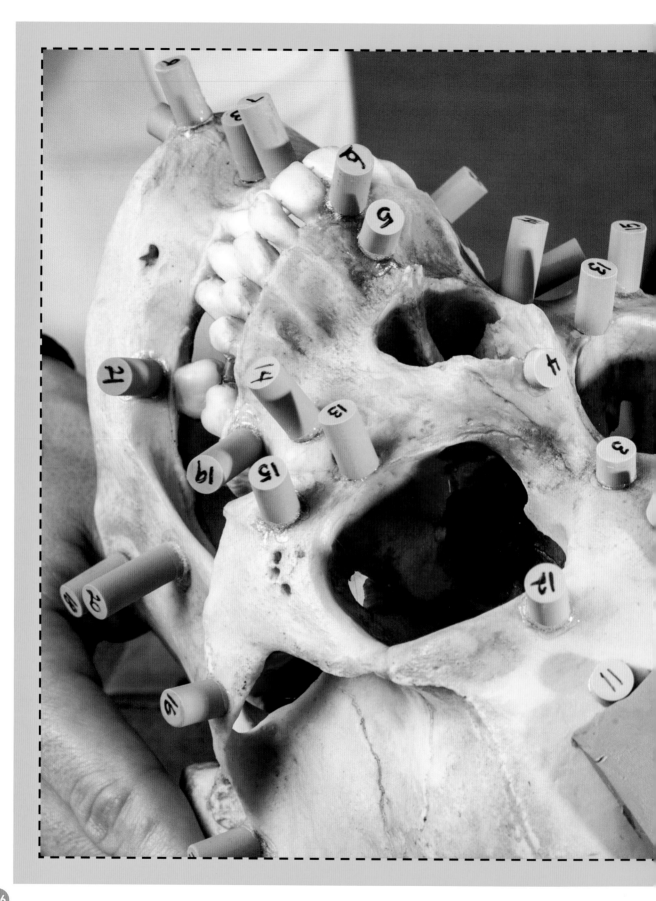

FORENSIC ANTHROPOLOGY

BUT WHOSE BONES ARE THEY ANYWAY? You set out to answer that question with Dr. Hena Patel and other forensic anthropologists who are brought in to make the ultimate determination. Carefully, you arrange the skeletal remains on a large table. First, the team of forensic anthropologists will need to determine how complete the skeleton is. The good news is that it looks like just about all of the bones are there. The team has no trouble determining what each of the bones are and how they fit together. Each bone in the human body has a distinctive shape, and bones remain intact for many years after a body is buried. Bones from different parts of a body offer researchers different kinds of information, and each one brings them closer to discovering whose skeleton this might be.

» **MAN OR WOMAN** One of the easiest things that a skeleton can tell you is whether the remains are from a male or female. The skull in a male has eye sockets that protrude more, meaning they stick out from the rest of the skull more than a female's eye sockets do. Also, the pelvis in a female has a wider opening at the base than a male pelvis. Right away, you determine that these bones belonged to a man.

» **YOUNG OR OLD** You can also get clues about the age of the person by looking at how the bones in the center of the upper part of the skull come together. In children, these bones haven't yet fused together, or attached to one another. That means that if the bones are connected, the person was an adult. That's the case here.

» **INJURIES** This particular skeleton has another interesting feature—a ridge-like area in the middle of one of the ribs. That's an indication that the person broke that bone at some point. Ridges like that tend to be created when a bone heals. You call Helen McCain to ask if her great-great uncle Theodore ever broke any bones. She mentions hearing a story about a broken leg when Theodore was a boy but nothing about a broken rib.

» **ETHNICITY** Skull and teeth characteristics can provide clues about the race of a person. Based on the shape of the top of the mouth, teeth, and nose of this skeleton, your forensic anthropologists are beginning to think that these remains might be Native American. If that's the case, the bones would be much older than if they belonged to McCain's great-great uncle. How old are they? Carbon dating will help you figure that out.

CARBON DATING

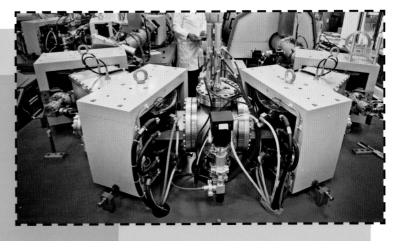

Dating bones involves examining the carbon in them. The element carbon comes in different forms. Two are helpful for dating old materials: Carbon-14 is a radioactive form of carbon, and carbon-12 is a nonradioactive form. Substances that are radioactive fall apart, or decay, because their atoms are unstable. When they decay, they become nonradioactive.

So how does that help us to date old bones? Carbon-14 exists in the atmosphere as part of the carbon dioxide (CO_2) molecules in the air. When CO_2 is used by plants for photosynthesis, both carbon-12 and carbon-14 become part of the plants' structure. People and other animals take in both kinds of carbon atoms when they eat plants. The level of carbon-14 in a person's body stays fairly consistent while they're alive. But after a person dies, the carbon-14 in their body begins to decay. By comparing the amount of carbon-12 to the amount of carbon-14 that has decayed, scientists can determine how long a person has been dead. In order to get that information, you'll need to put a sample of the bone through an instrument called an accelerated mass spectrometer.

ACCELERATED MASS SPECTROMETER

The accelerated mass spectrometer speeds up all the particles from the bone and separates them by weight. Because carbon-14 is heavier than carbon-12, this separation allows you to compare the amount of the two in your bone sample. The less carbon-14 in the sample, the older the bone.

✷ AND THE RESULTS SHOW ... ✷

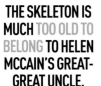

THE SKELETON IS MUCH TOO OLD TO BELONG TO HELEN MCCAIN'S GREAT-GREAT UNCLE.

The analysis comes back with a carbon date of 9,000 years, which means this skeleton belonged to a Native person, most likely an ancestor of the modern-day Tribe living in the region. Based on this investigation, the museum returns the bones to the Tribe, and Max Williams works with the Tribal Historic Preservation Officer to organize a quiet and private reburial in the presence of a few Tribal citizens. The location is kept secret to ensure that this time, the bones stay buried. The following week, a court orders that construction on the Purple Meadow Properties site be halted indefinitely, until a team of archaeologists can work with Tribal leaders to determine if the location is indeed a larger Native burial ground.

Williams pins a local newspaper article about the discovery on the bulletin board at the Tribe's cultural center. Beside it, he posts a response from Tribal leaders. It notes the importance of the Native American Graves Protection and Repatriation Act and their objection to Native remains being displayed in museums or being subjected to scientific testing. It explains that these acts are against their beliefs and are considered disrespectful. It is their hope that if more bones are discovered at the construction site, they'll be reburied immediately.

A CLOSER LOOK

TRACE EVIDENCE

TRACE EVIDENCE REFERS TO PIECES OF EVIDENCE SO TINY THAT EXPERTS MOST OFTEN USE MICROSCOPES TO STUDY THEM. The very first microscope is believed to have been invented around 1590, by a Dutch father and son named Hans and Zacharias Janssen, who also made spectacles, or eyeglasses. Their early microscope consisted of two lenses in a brass tube, and it could magnify things so they appeared to be three to nine times their real size.

Robert Hooke experimented with early microscopes in the 1600s, and he wrote a book called *Micrographia* with sketches of things he'd viewed under the microscope. In 1675, Dutch scientist Antonie van Leeuwenhoek made a hand-held microscope with a single lens, which he used to observe insects and other specimens. Later, he'd be the first person to observe bacteria under a microscope.

Image of red seaweed cells taken by Robert Hooke

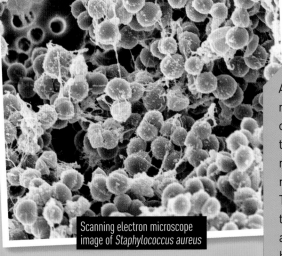

Scanning electron microscope image of *Staphylococcus aureus*

As time passed, people made more powerful microscopes. By the 1800s, microscopes with comparison bridges allowed scientists to look at two samples, side by side. The scanning electron microscope, developed in 1938, gave scientists a much closer, and clearer, look at their specimens. Today's microscopes offer magnification of up to 300,000 times larger than the actual object, allowing forensic scientists to see blood cells, hair, fiber, and pollen grains.

Real-World
CRIME SCIENCE!

In 1993, a man named Charles Smithart was spotted near the scene of a crime in Alaska. Investigators didn't have any other evidence to connect him to the crime. But they did find tiny bits of metal on the victim's clothing. Forensic scientists studied that trace evidence under a scanning electron microscope and found that the iron bits had a unique shape to them—one that's only created by welding or grinding. It turned out that Smithart had a welding rig where he fixed bikes for local kids. That evidence, along with some fiber evidence, led to his conviction.

Another kind of trace evidence, pollen, was used to solve the case of a New Zealand crime in 2008. At first, police didn't have any suspects in the case. They had almost no real evidence. What they did have was pollen from the victim's body and clothing. So the police reached out to a forensic palynologist, someone who studies pollen and spores as they relate to crimes. This expert found that some of the pollen grains from the victim had an unusual characteristic. Instead of one pore, like most pollen grains have, these had two. The expert wondered if an herbicide, a

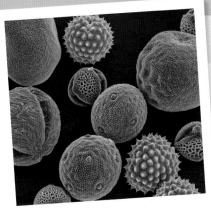

Photo of pollen grains

chemical used to kill unwanted plants, had caused that mutation, or change, in the pollen.

The police had been wondering about something, too. There was a local gang that hung out in a warehouse area near where the victim was found. Could one of those gang members be responsible for the crime? The pollen clue convinced them that their hunch might be right. Those weird, two-pored pollen grains were found near the warehouse area, too. It turns out that area had been sprayed with herbicides. The pollen grains were a match, and police had determined where the crime took place, and they eventually arrested the guilty gang member.

DISCOVER HOW AN ACCELERATED MASS SPECTROMETER WORKS

An accelerated mass spectrometer is essential in the process of carbon dating because it separates carbon-14 and carbon-12 particles. That allows scientists to count them and determine the ratio between the two. Here's a fun experiment you can try at home to see how this machine works.

>> WHAT YOU'LL NEED

- a three-ring binder and two hardcover books with flat spines

- A hair dryer

- Books, rulers, or other materials to create a wall

- About 30 pennies (representing carbon-12)

- About 15 nickels (representing carbon-14)

!

ADULT SUPERVISION REQUIRED:

Use of hot-air source

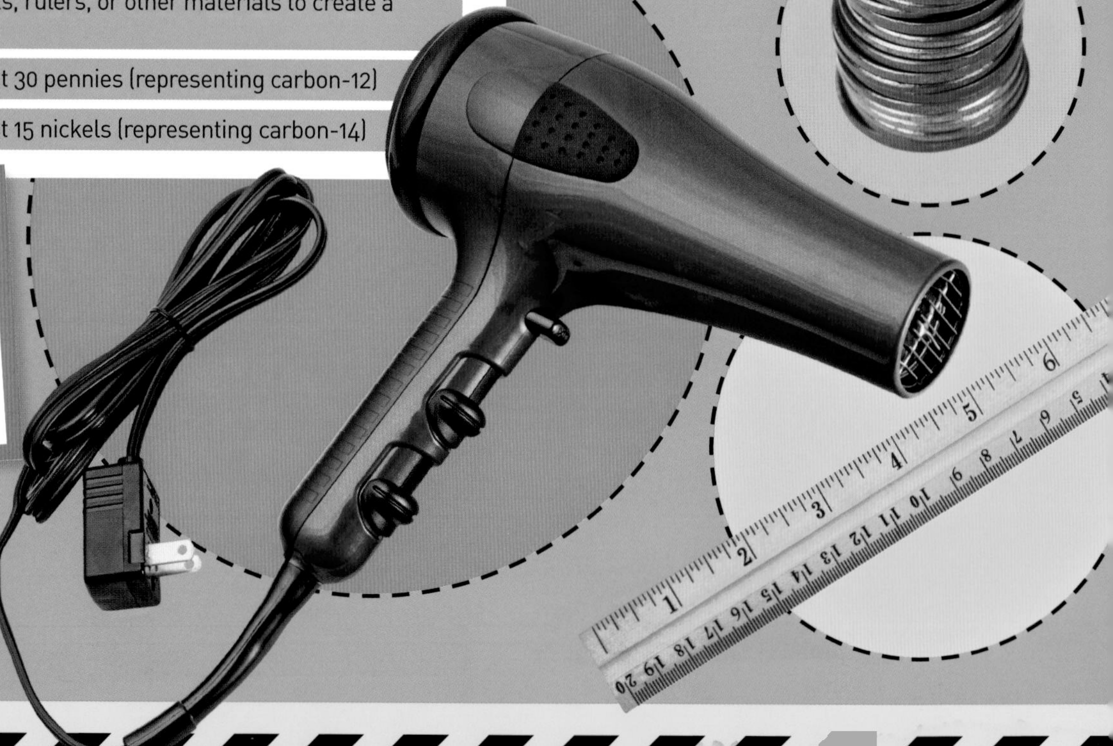

>> PROCEDURE

1 Place the binder on a hard, flat surface like a table or wooden floor to make a ramp. Be sure to set it up near an electrical outlet.

2 Place the two books on the ramp, spines facing each other, and spaced apart just enough to insert a coin to roll down the ramp.

3 Plug in your hair dryer and lay it on its side so that it's blowing across the path the coins will take after they roll down the ramp. It should be six to eight inches (15 to 20 cm) past the end of the ramp. The hair dryer will be blowing the coins off to the side after they leave the ramp.

4 Set up a little wall or blockade of some kind a few feet away to stop the coins after they've turned. A row of books or rulers will work fine for this.

5 Turn on the hair dryer and, one by one, roll your coins on their edge down the ramp. The force of the air coming from the hair dryer will cause the coins to turn.

6 When you're out of coins, check out the two piles. Did one kind of coin usually turn before the other? Which turned more quickly? What might account for this?

>> HOW IT WORKS

You'll find that the pennies, which are lighter than the nickels, turn sooner. The heavier nickels will take a little longer to turn, so this process separates the coins into piles based on their weight. The same thing happens in a mass spectrometer, which uses an electric field to accelerate the particles and a magnetic field to cause them to turn. In your simulation, the acceleration comes from the force of gravity as the coins roll down the ramp. Your hair dryer takes the place of the magnetic field, causing the coins to turn and separate by weight.

1–4

5

6

SO YOU WANT TO BE A FORENSIC SCIENTIST!

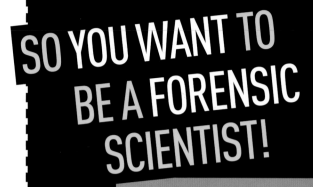

>> **WERE YOU AN ACE WHEN IT CAME TO SOLVING THE MYSTERIES IN THIS BOOK? DOES FORENSIC SCIENCE SOUND EXCITING AND INTERESTING TO YOU AS A CAREER?** Here are some of the skills and education you'll need to be successful. Science, math, and language arts are all important subjects for the future forensic scientist. You'll need to have a solid background in all of the related branches of science, and you'll also need excellent communication skills. Taking detailed, accurate notes is an essential part of a forensic scientist's job, and so is writing clear reports. As a forensic scientist, the chances are good that you'll also need to testify in court someday, so speaking skills are important, too.

Typically, forensic scientists study science in college but also have a strong background in math, statistics, and writing. Some jobs in the field of forensic science also require an advanced degree and specialized training. Most of all, this field requires curiosity and excellent observation skills. And that's something you can practice every day. Go outside. Observe. Write or draw observations in a notebook. And don't be afraid to ask questions. Every scientific discovery, every solved crime, and every solution to a problem begins with curiosity.

GLOSSARY

AFIS (AUTOMATED FINGERPRINT IDENTIFICATION SYSTEM):
a methodology that uses digital imaging to collect, store, and analyze fingerprint data

ANALYSIS:
a detailed examination of something that involves breaking it down into smaller parts to better understand it

BIOLOGY:
the study of living things and how they interact

BLOOD SPATTER ANALYSIS:
the study and analysis of bloodstains at a crime scene to help investigators learn details about the crime, including how and when it happened

BLOOD TYPE:
classification of blood based on the presence of certain protein markers on the surface of red blood cells; in humans, there are four basic blood types: A, B, AB, and O

BOTANY:
the study of plants

BUNSEN BURNER:
a small burner, used in laboratories, that produces a single open gas flame

CARBON DATING:
a method of determining the age of organic matter

CARRIER GAS:
a gas, usually helium, used in the process of gas-liquid chromatography

CELL:
the basic building blocks of all living things, and the smallest unit of life that can reproduce on its own

CELL MEMBRANE:
a thin double layer of fats and proteins that surrounds a cell and protects it from its surroundings but allows certain molecules like oxygen and water to flow through

CENTRIFUGE:
a piece of laboratory equipment that spins liquid samples at high speeds, most often for the purpose of separating liquids from solids or separating fluids of different densities

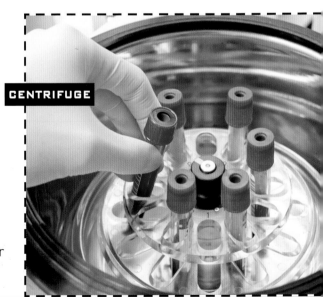

CENTRIFUGE

CHEMISTRY:
the study of matter and how chemical reactions occur

CHROMOSOMES:
threadlike structures that carry genetic information in DNA and are found in the nucleus of most living cells

CODIS (COMBINED DNA INDEX SYSTEM):
an FBI system of software and databases that lets federal, state, and local forensic laboratories compare DNA samples electronically

DATABASE:
a collection of data or information held in a computer and typically organized for quick search and retrieval

DECOMPOSITION:
the process by which once-living substances, including bodies, are broken down into smaller pieces via decay, or rotting

DNA (DEOXYRIBONUCLEIC ACID):
the material that carries genetic information in all living things

EAR PRINT:
a unique print created when a person's outer ear comes in contact with a surface

ECOLOGY:
the study of where organisms live, how many there are, and how they are affected by their environment

EXEMPLAR:
a typical example of something, such as handwriting

DNA STRAND

EVIDENCE:
all of the available information that can be used to prove whether or not something is true

FBI (FEDERAL BUREAU OF INVESTIGATION):
the main federal law enforcement agency in the United States

FINGERPRINT:
a unique impression left by the ridges of a human finger

FORENSIC ANTHROPOLOGIST:
a scientist who studies human remains for the purpose of gathering details about cause of death and other information

FORENSIC ENTOMOLOGIST:
a scientist who studies insects on decomposing bodies for the purpose of gathering details about time of death and other information

FORENSIC SCIENCE:
the application of science to laws, most often relating to criminal investigations

FTIR (FOURIER TRANSFORM INFRARED) SPECTROMETER:
an instrument that exposes an unknown substance to infrared light, creates a graph of how the sample interacts with it, and compares that graph to a library of known materials

IP ADDRESS

INFRARED LIGHT:
a type of light that is invisible to the human eye and can be used as part of a process to identify unknown substances

INK CHROMATOGRAPHY:
a process that separates the colored pigments contained in ink for analysis

IP ADDRESS:
a string of numbers that identifies a device connected to a computer network

MATTER:
any substance that has mass and takes up space

MEDULLA:
the innermost part of a tissue, such as a hair

METEOROLOGY:
the study of the atmosphere, weather, and forecasting the weather

MOLECULE:
a group of atoms held together by chemical bonds, creating the smallest unit of a compound that can take part in a chemical reaction

NUCLEAR MEMBRANE:
the membrane that surrounds the genetic material in the nucleus of a cell

OCEANOGRAPHY:
the study of Earth's oceans and seas

ORGANISM:
a single life-form, such as an animal, plant, or single-celled life-form

GC-MS (GAS CHROMATOGRAPH–MASS SPECTROMETER):
an instrument used in laboratories to separate a sample into its chemical components

GENETIC:
relating to inherited traits in living organisms

GEOLOGY:
the study of Earth, what it is made of, and how it changes over time

HEMOGLOBIN:
a protein that carries oxygen and is found in the red blood cells of vertebrates

IMPRESSION:
a mark created when one object comes in contact with another, such as shoeprints, tire prints, toolmarks, and bite marks

INDICATOR:
a substance that turns a specific color in the presence of a certain material

PHENOLPHTHALEIN:
an indicator that turns hot pink in the presence of blood

PHOTOSYNTHESIS:
the process by which green plants use sunlight, carbon dioxide, and water to make food

PROTEIN:
large molecules that are part of living organisms

RADIOACTIVE SUBSTANCE:
a substance that falls apart, or decays, over time because its atoms are unstable

RUVIS (REFLECTED ULTRAVIOLET IMAGING SYSTEM):
a device that uses ultraviolet light to detect fingerprints on nonporous surfaces

SALINE:
a solution of salt in water

SALIVA:
watery liquid secreted by glands in the mouth (also known as spit)

SEDATIVE:
a drug that induces calmness or sleep

SOLVENT:
a substance used to dissolve other substances

TOXICOLOGY:
a scientific specialty that deals with poisons

ULTRAVIOLET LIGHT:
also called black light, this is light with a specific wavelength that can be used to detect tiny amounts of evidence like blood or hair in forensic investigations

ZOOLOGY:
a branch of biology that specializes in the animal kingdom

FINGERPRINTS UNDER UV LIGHT

MORE RESOURCES

If you'd like to learn more about forensic science, check out the following resources.

BOOKS

For a great story about the work of forensic anthropologists, check out *Written in Bone: Buried Lives of Jamestown and Colonial Maryland* by Sally Walker (Carolrhoda Books, 2009).

Check out the series Forensics: The Science of Crime-Solving (Mason Crest Publishers), which includes the following titles:

- *Computer Investigation* by Elizabeth Bauchner
- *Document Analysis* by Elizabeth Bauchner
- *Explosives and Arson Investigation* by Jean Ford
- *Fingerprints, Bite Marks, Ear Prints* by Angela Libal
- *Forensics in American Culture: Obsessed with Crime* by Jean Otto Ford
- *Mark and Trace Analysis* by William Hunter
- *Solving Crimes with Physics* by William Hunter

Another series, called Crime Scene Investigations (Gale, Cengage Learning), also looks at elements of forensic science:

- *The Crime Scene Photographer* by Gail B. Stewart
- *Underwater Forensics* by Gail B. Stewart

WEBSITES

HowStuffWorks has a whole section dedicated to the branches of forensic science:
- science.howstuffworks.com/forensic-science -channel.htm

A Simplified Guide to Forensic Science offers explanations of everything from fingerprinting to toxicology:
- forensicsciencesimplified.org

"GCMS—How Does It Work?" from the Oregon State University Environmental Health Sciences Center provides a clear explanation on the workings of the gas chromatograph–mass spectrometer:
- unsolvedmysteries.oregonstate.edu/MS_05

The TED-Ed video "What Is DNA and How Does It Work?" by Wendy Vidor explains the science of DNA:
- ed.ted.com/on/rGgl3J5s

The accelerated mass spectrometer experiment on page 142 of this book is courtesy of Dr. Erica Saint Clair of Rosie Research and is shared here with her permission. You can see Dr. Erica's video demonstration of the nickels-and-pennies simulation here:
- youtube.com/watch?v=rIHMLREt8kE

Check out more of her science projects for kids at
- rosieresearch.com

The Stolen Bones mystery in this book was inspired by the real-life story of the Kennewick Man, whose remains were found in Washington State, U.S.A., in 1996. You can read the story of how forensic anthropologists determined whose bones had been unearthed in the article "Over 9,000 Years Later, Kennewick Man Will Be Given a Native American Burial" from *Smithsonian* magazine.
- smithsonianmag.com/smart-news/over -9000-years-later-kennewick-man-will-be -given-native-american-burial-180958947

Carolyn McClellan, former assistant director of programs at the Smithsonian's National Museum of the American Indian, also assisted with this mystery. She previously served as the Native American Graves Protection and Repatriation Act Coordinator for the Bureau of Indian Affairs. You can read more about this law that protects Native graves here:
- nps.gov/history/tribes/documents/nagpra.pdf

SOURCES

Bowen, Robin, and Jessica Schneider. "Forensic Databases: Paint, Shoe Prints, and Beyond." National Institute of Justice, nij.gov/journals/258/pages /forensic-databases.aspx.

Ferlini, Roxana. *Silent Witness: How Forensic Anthropology Is Used to Solve the World's Toughest Crimes.* Firefly Books, 2002.

Freeman, Shanna. "How Forensic Dentistry Works: Bite-Mark Analysis." HowStuffWorks, science .howstuffworks.com/forensic-dentistry3.htm.

Hallcox, Jarrett, and Amy Welch. *Bodies We've Buried: Inside the National Forensic Academy, the World's Top CSI Training School.* Berkley Books, 2006.

McDermid, Val. *Forensics: What Bugs, Burns, Prints, DNA, and More Tell Us About Crime.* Grove Press, 2015.

Mosher, Dave. "Ears Could Make Better Unique IDs Than Fingerprints." *Wired,* November 12, 2010, wired .com/2010/11/ears-biometric-identification.

National Forensic Science Technology Center. "A Simplified Guide to Footwear & Tire Track Examination." forensicsciencesimplified.org/fwtt /FootwearTireTracks.pdf.

Owen, David. *Hidden Evidence: Forty True Crimes and How Forensic Science Helped Solve Them.* Firefly Books, 2000.

Ramsland, Katherine. *The C.S.I. Effect.* Berkley Books, 2006.

Reaney, Patricia. "Scientists Get Computerized Grip on Ear Prints." NBCNews.com, March 8, 2004, nbcnews .com/id/4482955/ns/technology_and_science -science/t/scientists-get-computerized-grip-ear -prints/#.W2NhgdhKj_Q.

Saferstein, Richard. *Forensic Science: An Introduction.* Pearson Education, 2011.

Scheve, Tom. "How Body Farms Work." HowStuffWorks, science.howstuffworks.com/body -farm1.htm.

Tilstone, William J., Kathleen A. Savage, and Leigh A. Clark. *Forensic Science: An Encyclopedia of History, Methods, and Techniques.* ABC-CLIO, 2006.

INDEX

Boldface indicates illustrations.

YOU'VE GOT THIS!

You'll be able to think your way through **ANYTHING** and have **FUN** doing it after you check out all the books in the awesome **THIS!** series. Each specially themed book is chock-full of hands-on activities and easy-to-follow instructions about real-world scenarios to help you build skills, confidence, and competence!

CREATIVE PROJECTS

ENGINEERING CHALLENGES

PROGRAMMING CONCEPTS

NATIONAL GEOGRAPHIC KIDS

CODE THIS!

PUZZLES, GAMES, CHALLENGES, AND COMPUTER CODING CONCEPTS FOR THE PROBLEM-SOLVER IN YOU!

JENNIFER SZYMANSKI

> BREAK IT DOWN

CODING CONCEPT: OPTIMIZATION

DECODING THE CONCEPT

If you've ever had to pack a bag for a long trip, you know that you can't take it all. You have to make some tough choices about what to bring, and what to leave behind. To do that, you have to ... that's right ... **optimize** the space in your bag by choosing the things you need most that will fit into your bag.

It's the same with coding. Though there are often many ways to write the same directions, shorter code will make the computer run more efficiently.

TRY OPTIMIZING THE BEST COMBINATION OF THINGS ON THIS PAGE. CAN YOU MAKE THE BEST CHOICES FOR A TRIP TO THE BEACH?

TRY IT OUT

CODY'S CAMP CHAIR

Jaguars are notoriously shy animals, so it might be some time before one feels safe enough to approach Cody's camp. Cody needs to be prepared to wait a while. **Can you construct a model of a chair** that's light and easy to fold up but roomy to ride Cody's cargo compartment but sturdy enough to hold Cody's weight?

WHAT YOU'LL NEED

- Paper and pencil
- A sandwich bag
- A potato or apple (to represent Cody)
- Scissors
- Tape
- Toothpicks
- Wooden craft sticks
- Plastic wrap
- Aluminum foil
- A piece of cloth about 3 inches (10 cm) square

WHAT TO DO

1 USE THE PIECE OF PAPER AND PENCIL TO SKETCH A FEW IDEAS FOR YOUR CHAIR. You model should be small enough to fit into the plastic baggie. You can fold your chair up to make it apart, as long as you can pull it back together when you "get" to the camp. Remember: You can only use the materials you have on the list!

CODY'S CAMP CHAIR continued

FUN EXPERIMENTS

PLANTS

RAINBOW ROSE

Color a white rose in rainbow shades.

CONCEPTS
PLANT STRUCTURES AND PROCESSES

HOW LONG IT TAKES

WHAT YOU NEED

W hat's a xylem? It's the system of cells inside a plant's roots and stem that transports water from ground or vase to the top of the plant. This project lets you discover what sections of the xylem feed what part.

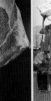

WHAT TO DO

NOTE ABOUT FOOD COLORING: This works best with the gel food coloring sold at cake supply shops.

QUESTION THIS!

- What accounts for different swaths of color?
- What happens if you leave the stem in the dye for longer than four days?
- What happens if you do this with a rose that has a natural color?

TRY THIS!

NATIONAL GEOGRAPHIC KIDS

50 FUN EXPERIMENTS FOR THE MAD SCIENTIST IN YOU

BY KAREN ROMANO YOUNG

SPECIAL F/X

ELEPHANT TOOTHPASTE

Can you replicate an extreme reaction?

SAFETY CHECK
TRICKY   WHO YOU NEED

SUPERVISION: CHEMICAL REACTIONS

CONCEPTS
CHEMISTRY

HOW LONG IT TAKES
30 minutes

WHAT YOU NEED

OUR TRY

We worked together to decide on the two colors we would mix the each bottle blue and green, blue and purple, red and yellow. Barron chose a clean pot handling chemicals made the plastic mixture to measure cup. The others cut foam handling chemicals. So protected by goggles, gloves, and aprons closed the seeds mixture into the bottles, and we all stood back to watch. The results, it "toothpaste" spurted and the bubbling shapes and textures, some of it foamed, massive the blue purpose mix. It overflowed the "spiked" and flowed into the trays. Then, quickly, the reaction slowed. The bubbles continued to move over the colors overcame the initial formation was over, so the dripping reaction could be observed.

WHAT TO DO

1 STAND soda bottle in foil pan.

2 INSERT FUNNEL in neck of bottle.

3 ADD ½ cup peroxide, detergent, and food coloring.

4 IN MEASURING CUP, dissolve yeast in ¼ cup of water. Combine with plastic spoon.

5 POUR YEAST mixture into soda bottle and remove funnel.

WARNING: Avoid touching or getting the chemicals on skin or clothing.

R eplication is an important part of science, if a scientist can't copy your procedure and get the same results, your science comes into questions. We had seen this reaction demonstrated on television and wanted to try it for ourselves.

"I feel like my hand—my water, but it's hardening on my fingers in the bottle it looked so much different than when it came out." —Barron

TRY THIS! EXTREME

NATIONAL GEOGRAPHIC KIDS

50 FUN & SAFE EXPERIMENTS FOR THE MAD SCIENTIST IN YOU

BY KAREN ROMANO YOUNG
PHOTOGRAPHS BY MATTHEW RAKOLA

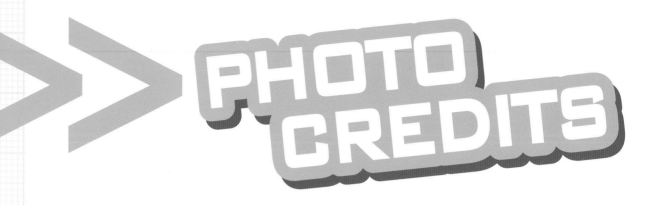

PHOTO CREDITS

All illustrations by Jason Tharpe unless otherwise noted below.

COVER: (dusting brush), Comaniciu Dan/Shutterstock; (red paint splatter), Oksanabratanova/Dreamstime; (fingerprint), Andrey_Kuzmin/Shutterstock; (computer), ifong/Shutterstock; (flashlight), CPM PHOTO/Shutterstock; (chipmunk), Dimj/Shutterstock; (hand), Microgen/Shutterstock; (footprints), Panptys/Shutterstock; **BACK COVER:** (microscope), BCFC/Shutterstock; (footprint cast), Jim Varney/Science Photo Library; (bonobo), Eric Isselee/Shutterstock; (foot prints), Panptys/Shutterstock

FRONT MATTER: 4 (UP LE), Oksanabratanova/Dreamstime; 4 (UP RT), paulaphoto/Shutterstock; 4 (CTR), Sylvia sooyoN/Shutterstock; 4 (LO), armpeti/Shutterstock; 5 (UP), dlerick/iStockphoto/Getty Images; 5 (CTR), Milan M/Shutterstock; 5 (LO), Sashkin/Shutterstock; 6-7, Fer Gregory/Shutterstock; 8 (UP LE), Jack Nevitt/Shutterstock; 8 (UP RT), Sailorr/Shutterstock; 8 (LO), Michal Ludwiczak/Shutterstock; 9 (UP LE), Francesco R. Iacomino/Shutterstock; 9 (UP RT), Christian Musat/Shutterstock; 9 (CTR LE), SpiffyJ/iStockphoto/Getty Images; 9 (CTR RT), Ludmila Ruzickova/Shutterstock; 9 (LO), Vlad61/Shutterstock; 10 (UP), Jason Butcher/Cultura RF/Getty Images; 10 (LO), dencg/Shutterstock; 11 (UP LE), Iudex/iStockphoto/Getty Images; 11 (UP RT), Corbis; 11 (LO RT), sakkmesterke/Shutterstock; 12 (UP LE), Sean Clarkson/Alamy Stock Photo; 12 (UP RT), Tek Image/Science Photo Library/Getty Images; 12 (LO), S Curtis/Shutterstock; 13 (UP), Eurelios/National Geographic Image Collection; 13 (LO LE), Jeff Thrower/Shutterstock; 13 (LO RT), DreamerAchieverNoraTarvus/Shutterstock; 14 (UP), paulaphoto/Shutterstock; 14 (LO), Ulrich Baumgarten/Getty Images; 15 (UP), Mauro Fermariello/Science Photo Library; 15 (LO), Gordana Sermek/Dreamstime; 16 (LE), Tek Image/Science Photo Library; 16 (RT), Science & Society Picture Library/Getty Images; 17 (LE), GIPhotoStock/Science Photo Library; 17 (UP RT), DisabilityImages/Getty Images; 17 (footprint database), Foster & Freeman Ltd; 17 (computer), zentilia/Shutterstock; 18 (UP), Gelpi/Shutterstock; 20, Gerisima/Shutterstock; 21 (UP), PhotoDISC; 21 (LO LE), Mega Pixel/Shutterstock; 21 (LO RT), Trinacria Photo/Shutterstock

CHAPTER 1: 24-25, Eric Lafforgue/Art In All Of Us/Corbis via Getty Images; 25 (small spiral top notebook), Alivepix/Shutterstock; 30 (UP), Oksanabratanova/Dreamstime; 30 (LO), Dabarti CGI/Shutterstock; 31 (UP), Tek Image/Science Photo Library; 31 (CTR), Savelov Maksim/Shutterstock; 31 (LO), alejandro dans neergaard/Shutterstock; 32, Sylvia sooyoN/Shutterstock; 33 (UP), Andrew Brookes/Cultura RF/Getty Images; 33 (INSET), Mikael Karlsson/Alamy Stock Photo; 33 (LO), Inked Pixels/Shutterstock; 34 (UP), Richard T. Nowitz/Science Photo Library; 34 (CTR), Richard T. Nowitz/Science Photo Library; 34 (LO), KRPD/Shutterstock; 35, Mikael Karlsson/Alamy Stock Photo; 36, marin_bulat/Shutterstock; 37 (UP LE), Billion Photos/Shutterstock; 37 (UP RT), Sean Clarkson/Alamy Stock Photo; 37 (LO), Ian Miles-Flashpoint Pictures/Alamy Stock Photo; 38 (UP), Ian Miles-Flashpoint Pictures/Alamy Stock Photo; 38 (LO), Jim Varney/Science Photo Library; 39, Mauro Fermariello/Science Photo Library; 40 (UP), Anteromite/Shutterstock; 40 (LO), DisabilityImages/Getty Images; 41 (UP), Designua/Shutterstock; 41 (LO LE), Biophoto Associates/Science Photo Library; 41 (LO RT), Volodymyr Nikitenko/Shutterstock; 42, Krisda/Shutterstock; 43 (UP), Dimedrol68/Shutterstock; 43 (LO), ronstik/Shutterstock; 44, Eric Lafforgue/Art In All Of Us/Corbis via Getty Images; 46, RTimages/Shutterstock; 47, livepix/Shutterstock; 48 (UP RT), thagoon/Shutterstock; 48 (UP LE), Don Farrall/Getty Images; 48 (LO), The History Collection/Alamy Stock Photo; 49 (UP LE), Historia/Shutterstock; 49 (UP RT), Sheila Terry/Science Photo Library; 49 (LO), Corbis via Getty Images; 50 (UP), Prakarn Pudtan/Shutterstock; 50 (CTR RT), Moving Moment/Shutterstock; 50 (CTR LE), photastic/Shutterstock; 50 (LO), Inked Pixels/Shutterstock; 51, Mark Thiessen, NGP Staff; 51 (LO), Everilda/Shutterstock

CHAPTER 2: 54, Alivepix/Shutterstock; 54-55, Frans Lanting/National Geographic Image Collection; 60 (LE), Sergey Uryadnikov/Shutterstock; 60 (RT), harmpeti/Shutterstock; 61 (UP), Phanie/Getty Images; 61 (LO), Richard T. Nowitz/

Science Photo Library; 62 (UP), AB Forces News Collection/Alamy Stock Photo; 62 (LO), Kalamurzing/Shutterstock; 63, RP Library/Alamy Stock Photo; 64, SergiyN/Shutterstock; 65, Pablo Paul/Alamy Stock Photo; 66 (HANDS), Nisakorn Neera/Shutterstock; 66 (NOTEBOOK), aopsan/Shutterstock; 68 (UP), Shutter_M/Shutterstock; 68 (LO), happydancing/Shutterstock; 68-69, Cphoto/Dreamstime; 69 (UP), sittipong/Shutterstock; 69 (LO LE), Helga Gavrilova/Shutterstock; 69 (LO RT), Pictac/iStockphoto; 70 (UP), Pictac/iStockphoto; 70 (CTR), sittipong/Shutterstock; 70 (LO), Helga Gavrilova/Shutterstock; 72 (LE), Jr images/Shutterstock; 72 (RT), Mauro Fermariello/Science Source; 73 (UP), David Alary/Shutterstock; 73 (LO (computer)), cobalt88/Shutterstock; 73 (LO INSET), Kevin L Chesson/Shutterstock; 76, RTimages/Shutterstock; 77, Alivepix/Shutterstock; 78 (UP LE), ImageZoo/Alamy Stock Photo; 78 (UP RT), thagoon/Shutterstock; 78 (LO), Maksym Azovtsev/Adobe Stock; 79 (UP), Library of Congress Prints and Photographs Division; 79 (LO LE), Bettmann Archive/Getty Images; 79 (LO RT), Keystone/Hulton Archive/Getty Images; 80 (UP), Nokz/Shutterstock; 80 (CTR), vincent noel/Shutterstock; 80 (LO LE), Unclenikola/Dreamstime; 80 (LO CTR), Spectral-Design/Shutterstock; 80 (LO LE), Trinacria Photo/Shutterstock; 81-83, Mark Thiessen/NGP Staff

CHAPTER 3: 86-87, nlentz1/iStockphoto/Getty Images; 87, Alivepix/Shutterstock; 92, (HAND), 168 STUDIO/Shutterstock; 92 (COTTON), vilax/Shutterstock; 93 (UP BOTH), Jim Varney/Science Source; 93 (LO), harmpeti/Shutterstock; 94, anyaivanova/Shutterstock; 95, isak55/Shutterstock; 96, Makovsky Art/Shutterstock; 97 (UP), LdF/iStockphoto/Getty Images; 97 (LO), Ted Kinsman/Science Source; 98, New Africa/Shutterstock; 99, Misha Beliy/Shutterstock; 100, xpixel/Shutterstock; 101 (UP), Anton Starikov/Shutterstock; 101 (CTR LE), Boris15/Shutterstock; 101 (CTR RT), Vladislav Havrilov/Shutterstock; 101 (LO LE), Jochen Tack/imageBROKER/Shutter/Shutterstock; 101 (LO RT), xpixel/Shutterstock; 102 (UP LE), ND700/Shutterstock; 102 (UP RT), marilyn barbone/Shutterstock; 102 (LO), Simona Olteanu/Shutterstock; 103, nayneung1/Shutterstock; 106, RTimages/Shutterstock; 107, Alivepix/Shutterstock; 108 (UP LE), vitstudio/Shutterstock; 108 (UP RT), thagoon/Shutterstock; 108 (LO LE), Science History Images/Alamy Stock Photo; 108 (LO RT), Science History Images/Alamy Stock Photo; 109 (UP LE), Science History Images/Alamy Stock Photo; 109 (UP RT), Science & Society Picture Library/Getty Images; 109 (LO), Zuma Press, Inc./Alamy Stock Photo; 110 (UP LE), vincent noel/Shutterstock; 110 (UP RT), Gts/Shutterstock; 110 (CTR LE), Designs Stock/Shutterstock; 110 (CTR), M. Unal Ozmen/Shutterstock; 110 (CTR RT), Judith Collins/Alamy Stock Photo; 110 (BOWL), rprongjai/Shutterstock; 110 (LO CTR), Aleksandr Pobedimskiy/Shutterstock; 110 (LO RT), exopixel/Shutterstock; 110 (LO LE), topseller/Shutterstock111, Mark Thiessen/NGP Staff; 112

(RT ALL), Mark Thiessen/NGP Staff; 112 (LE), SOMMAI/Shutterstock; 113 (ALL), Mark Thiessen/NGP Staff

CHAPTER 4: 116, Alivepix/Shutterstock; 116-117, Rudmer Zwerver/Shutterstock; 119, aSuruwataRi/Shutterstock; 124 (UP), Milan M/Shutterstock; 124 (LO), Richard T. Nowitz/Science Source; 125 (UP), Richard T. Nowitz/Science Source; 125 (LO), Dimitris Leonidas/Shutterstock; 126, Avalon/Photoshot License/Alamy Stock Photo; 127 (UP), Cherdchai Chaivimol/Shutterstock; 127 (LO), NLM/Science Source; 128, Philippe Psaila/Science Source; 129, NLM/Science Source; 130, Regreto/Shutterstock; 131 (UP LE), Dennis Kunkel Microscopy/Science Source; 131 (UP RT), Sashkin/Shutterstock; 131 (LO LE), ggw/Shutterstock; 131 (LO RT), Tarzhanova/Shutterstock; 134, RTimages/Shutterstock; 135, Alivepix/Shutterstock; 136-137, Richard T. Nowitz/Science Source; 138 (UP), Sergio Azenha/Alamy Stock Photo; 138 (LO), Richard T. Nowitz/Science Source; 139, James King-Holmes/Science Source; 140 (UP LE), Science Source/Getty Images; 140 (UP RT), thagoon/Shutterstock; 140 (LO LE), Science Source/Getty Images; 140 (LO RT), Science Source/Getty Images; 141 (UP), Microspectacular/Shutterstock; 141 (LO), David Scharf/Science Source; 142 (UP), studioVin/Shutterstock; 142 (CTR), Eldad Carin/iStockphoto; 142 (LO LE), Photodisc; 142 (LO RT), SmileStudio/Shutterstock; 143, Mark Thiessen/NGP Staff; 144-145, Fer Gregory/Shutterstock; 145, Jacob Lund/Shutterstock

BACK MATTER: 146, T-Photo/Shutterstock; 147, Dabarti CGI/Shutterstock; 149, Andrew Brookes/Cultura RF/Getty Images; 150, LanKS/Shutterstock; various (ripped paper & tape), vesna cvorovic/Shutterstock; various (ripped paper), totally out/Shutterstock

For our parents, Tom and Gail Schirmer, who taught us to wonder. —KM, AR

ACKNOWLEDGMENTS

The authors and publisher wish to thank the Erie County Central Police Services Forensic Laboratory in Buffalo, New York, especially lab director Michelli Schmitz and DNA Technical Leader Tom Grille; Carolyn McClellan, former assistant director of programs at the Smithsonian's National Museum of the American Indian; Dr. Erica Saint Clair of Rosie Research; Mary Quattlebaum, for her careful read of the book; and the book team: Shelby Lees, senior editor; Lori Epstein, photo director; Sanjida Rashid, designer; Molly Reid, production editor; and Anne LeongSon and Gus Tello, production designers.

Since 1888, the National Geographic Society has funded more than 12,000 research, exploration, and preservation projects around the world. The Society receives funds from National Geographic Partners, LLC, funded in part by your purchase. A portion of the proceeds from this book supports this vital work. To learn more, visit natgeo.com/info.

For more information, visit nationalgeographic.com, call 1-877-873-6846, or write to the following address:

National Geographic Partners
1145 17th Street N.W.
Washington, D.C. 20036-4688 U.S.A.

Visit us online at nationalgeographic.com/books

For librarians and teachers: nationalgeographic.com/books/librarians-and-educators/

More for kids from National Geographic:
natgeokids.com

National Geographic Kids magazine inspires children to explore their world with fun yet educational articles on animals, science, nature, and more. Using fresh storytelling and amazing photography, *Nat Geo Kids* shows kids ages 6 to 14 the fascinating truth about the world—and why they should care.
kids.nationalgeographic.com/subscribe

For rights or permissions inquiries, please contact National Geographic Books Subsidiary Rights: bookrights@natgeo.com

Designed by Sanjida Rashid

Library of Congress Cataloging-in-Publication Data
Names: Messner, Kate, author. | Ruppert, Anne, author. | National Geographic Society (U.S.) | National Geographic Kids (Firm), publisher.
Title: Solve this : forensics / by Kate Messner and Anne Ruppert.
Other titles: Forensics
Description: Washington, DC : National Geographic Kids, [2020] | Audience: Ages 8-12. | Audience: Grades 4 to 6.
Identifiers: LCCN 2019007820| ISBN 9781426337444 (pbk.) | ISBN 9781426337451 (hardcover)
Subjects: LCSH: Science--Experiments--Juvenile literature. | Forensic sciences--Juvenile literature. | Problem solving--Juvenile literature. | Criminal investigation--Juvenile literature.
Classification: LCC Q164 .M47 2020 | DDC 507.8--dc23
LC record available at https://lccn.loc.gov/2019007820

Printed in Hong Kong
20/PPHK/1